THE CHURCH IN THE WORLD

Georgetown University Colloquium on the Church in the Modern World, 1966.

The Church in The World

X

Edited *by* CHARLES P. O'DONNELL

THE BRUCE PUBLISHING COMPANY/MILWAUKEE

NIHIL OBSTAT:

JOHN E. TWOMEY, S.T.L., PH.D.
Censor librorum

IMPRIMATUR:

✠ WILLIAM E. COUSINS
Archbishop of Milwaukee
July 24, 1967

Library of Congress Catalog Card Number: 67-28888

© 1967 GEORGETOWN UNIVERSITY
MADE IN THE UNITED STATES OF AMERICA

TO THOSE WHO WISH TO SEE THE CHURCH
WORK WITH THE WORLD
AND THE WORLD WITH THE CHURCH

Charles P. O'Donnell

This volume is one of the results of the Colloquium on the *Church in the Modern World* held at Georgetown University in July, 1966. The Colloquium brought together some thirty-five religious and laymen, of whom several had attended the sessions of Vatican II and others had given time and thought to the work of the Council, in particular to the *Pastoral Constitution on the Church in the Modern World* (herein referred to as the *Constitution*).

The participants viewed the *Constitution* from several perspectives. There were those whose primary interests were in the long-range philosophical and theological implications of the Council's work; others regarded the document as essentially a basis for operations. Some insisted on a single approach to the document. Others attacked the legalism and institutionalism of the Church and thought that the *Constitution* spoke to them in this vein. Others defended the continuing need for institutional structures, while agreeing that many existing ones should be drastically altered. There were those for whom the principal message of the document was the transformation of the world through the spirit of Christ.

Among the many specific topics touched on during the Colloquium were civil rights and their meaning for Catholics, Vietnam, the apathy of the laity, the dissatisfaction of the clergy, and the relationship of the Church to nationalism and nation-building. On a broader scale, much concern was expressed about the problems of missionaries, of Catholic universities, of

the family in our society, etc. Economic problems, the development of political institutions, especially in developing countries, the issue of nuclear deterrence and of the morality of
war, the need for an international organization of the family of
nations, and the role of the layman in the Church and in the
world were also topics heatedly discussed.

The Colloquium was made possible by the financial and
administrative support and cooperation of the Georgetown
Summer School and in particular of its dean, Dr. Rocco Porreco. The Most Reverend Edward J. Herrmann, D.D., Vicar-
General, Archdiocese of Washington, and Reverend George H.
Dunne, S.J., Assistant to the President, Georgetown University,
contributed to the work of the Colloquium. Its success owes
a great deal to the administration and faculty of Georgetown
University who offered their services in several capacities, and
especially to Professor Jean-Robert Leguey-Fuellieux.

The speakers, whose papers have been assembled and edited
for inclusion in this volume, were the following:

The Most Reverend John J. Wright, D.D., Bishop of Pittsburgh; The Right Reverend George G. Higgins, Director, Social
Action Department, United States Catholic Council, Washington, D.C.; Reverend John Courtney Murray, S.J., Woodstock
College, Woodstock, Md.; Reverend Francis X. Murphy, C.SS.R.,
Academia Alfonsiana, Rome; Reverend John L. Thomas, S.J.,
Research Associate, Cambridge Center for Social Studies,
Cambridge, Mass.; Dr. George N. Schuster, Assistant to the
President, Notre Dame University, Notre Dame, Ind.; Dr. John
J. Murphy, Department of Economics, Catholic University of
America, Washington, D.C.; Dr. Victor Ferkiss, Department of
Government, Georgetown University, Washington, D.C.; Dr.
William V. O'Brien, Chairman, Institute of World Polity, Georgetown University; Dr. Arnold Kaufman, Department of Philosophy, University of Michigan, Ann Arbor, Mich.; Professor John
Figueroa, Head of the Department of Education, University of
the West Indies.

One of the great themes of the Council as a whole, and most

particularly a theme of the *Constitution* — was the decision of
the Council to lend its support to a Christian humanism. This
decision could give timely and persuasive backing to the idea
of a secular city — a City of Man. This enunciation of a favorable view of the secular city could foreshadow a revolution of
many sorts for the Church and not less for political society
itself. Such a revolution could mean a decision for responsible
freedom rather than a preference for authoritarian pronouncements. It encourages a move toward a more egalitarian and
generous conception of the way men should live in society and
a move away from a class-conscious or autocratic mode of rul-
ing. It signifies a willingness to explore new avenues of knowledge and new styles of political thought and action. It rejects
the temptation to interpret historically limited interpretations
of ideas and action as though they were universal absolutes.
Such a revolution would mean that an awareness of the admixture of good and evil which creates so many tensions in
society and influences man's future so much need not lead to
hatred or disdain for the world. The revolution would be an
option for a spirituality ready to assist man in his daily life
here and now. In sum, the revolution proposes a secular city
open to the influences of the Church and its people — the
People of God — if they but rise to the occasion.

Father John Courtney Murray, in an earlier discussion of
Christian humanism, warned us of the difficulties of reconciling
the two versions of Christian humanism accepted in the Church.
The first, owing its strength to the thinking of St. Augustine, is
an other-worldly perspective on human affairs, triumphalist in
its aberrant and most common form. The second type of humanism consists in a profound Christian concern for the world and
its well-being, and a desire of Christians to bring to it their
spiritual strength. Those who hold this version are ill at ease
in a Church whose atmosphere is triumphalist. These human-
isms were in tension with one another in the Council. In spite
of the *Constitution's* deep concern with the welfare of men
here and now, the spirit of its kind of humanism will take a

very long time to permeate the Church and the world. Thorough-going pessimists think that the Church has been captured by ultra-conservatives and is dominated by institutions which thwart change. They hold that the *Constitution* will not inspire any great changes in the life of the Church or the world. The hopeful ones believe that a secular city open to religion can be accomplished, admittedly only after long and arduous work. Not least among the obstacles is the fact of the Christian diaspora and the unbelief of the present leadership of a large part of the world.

I believe it may be a good thing that the Church and the secular city remain in a state of tension. So enormous are the temptations of power in the hands of human beings that, given the divergencies of ultimate purposes, an intellectual attempt to reconcile differences could mean only a papering over of conflicting ambitions. Nor would mere compromise solutions, of which pragmatists are so fond, tend other than to episodic renewals of the struggle between embittered contestants, each seeking to serve the well-being of man. If we discard these alternatives, we should seek a healthy competitiveness, reckoning with differences and coping with the more serious ones as they arise. In this way we would preserve the integrity of the principle of the autonomy and independence of the Church and of political society.

I cannot agree with a pre-World War I view of Christopher Dawson that

> Christ came not to bring peace but a sword and the Kingdom of God comes not by the elimination of conflict but through an increasing opposition and tension between the Church and the World. The conflict between the two cities is as old as humanity and must endure to the end of time. (Christopher Dawson, *The Dynamics of World History,* edited by John J. Mulloy [New York: Mentor, 1962]. The quotation is from a symposium volume published in 1936 by Allen and Unwin.)

That there will be "tensions" between the two cities is certain,

but that there is to be "increasing opposition" and perpetual conflict is to bring Christians and non-Christians alike to the brink
of despair, and to tempt conflict. In the political or existential
dimensions of the relations between the city of God and the
city of Man, Christians in the spirit of Vatican II will at least
hope for "coexistence," possibly for "peaceful engagement" and,
even, for a more than wistful prospect of a future civilization
inspired by Christian ideals — a new Christendom.

CONTENTS

THE CHURCH IN THE WORLD

CHAPTER I

THE THRUST OF THE COUNCIL

The Most Reverend John J. Wright, D.D.

In what direction, even if we do not yet see it clearly, must we judge the Church to be moving in these predestined times? Whither are the prevailing winds of the Spirit blowing? What in a word, is the authentic "thrust" of the Second Vatican Council?

A general normative answer to this third question, which sums up the first two, seems warranted by no little evidence. That "thrust" underwent superficial changes during the course of the Council itself, though its more profound orientation, appointed by Divine Providence itself, was probably secure and certain from the beginning could one but know the counsel of God.

In the first session, the perspective of the Council was, in no small degree, toward the *past*. The clear intent was to encourage "dialogue" (the awkward, current word for decent Christian *conversation*) among the divided traditions of Christendom in the *present;* but the look was to the *past.* There was much talk about the tragic divisions of the sixteenth and seventeenth centuries; people speculated on what would have been the reactions of the sixteenth century and the period of the Protestant revolutions to the sheer goodness of Pope John XXIII and the ecumenical spirit of Vatican Council II. What would Luther and his German princes have done had vernacular liturgies been granted then as they are now? Would the sad divisions in Christendom have taken place as they did? The Lutheran Bishop of Berlin, Dr. Dibelius, and the American Cardinal Cushing both thought *not,* but the point is academic and the discussion was and is largely nostalgic, wistful, and romantic; moreover, it leaves out too much history and plain theological substance to be taken seriously for good and all.

Nonetheless, this was, in marked degree, the mood of the first session and no small part of the second. It was symbolized by the excitement over the presence of so many and such sincere non-Catholic delegate-observers; by the ecumenical preoccupations with which the first Council documents reported on the floor were (properly enough) read, debated, and (on occasion) rejected; by the central importance attached to the opinions of the Secretariate for Christian Unity; by the personal (and deserved) pre-eminence of Cardinal Bea; and by the response among all Christians to the pilgrimage of Pope Paul to those shrines of the Holy Land equally and universally cherished in Orthodox tradition, Protestant hymnody, and Catholic faith. (Pope John had made his prayerful pilgrimages on the eve of the Council to Italy's beloved sanctuaries of St. Francis and of the Holy House of Loreto).

The first session perspective had, then, dimensions deep in the *past* and largely focused on "dialogue" plus reform in the *present.*

But with the third session (really, already within the second) the perspective broadened immeasurably. It remained essentially Christian ecumenical; it could not do otherwise. It still fostered and depended upon present dialogue and reform; these, too, remained of the essence. But new dimensions were demanded and new frontiers were opened up with the establishment of the Secretariate for Non-Christian Religions, with the heightened appreciation of the long-range spiritual possibilities (as opposed to the short-range polemical exigencies) of the dialogue between Christians and Jews, as well as the other "people of the Book," and between the great world of Oriental religions and of all who seek Jesus Christ *in any way* or believe in God *at all.* This new thrust of the Council gathered incalculable momentum in, at, and after Pope Paul's dramatic visit to Bombay, symbol of a world that had hardly heard of our sixteenth century or of our Reformation and Counter-Reformation worthies, a world for whom any present religious encounters must be seen not as a search for lost graces and unities, but as the beginning of a search for future unities and undreamed blessings destined yet to be.

Yet even this does not suggest the final (and, I believe, permanent) thrust of the Council as this was to become, in the fourth session, as clear as God's hidden plans can possibly be in the midst of man's work and man's confusions. That further perspective of the Council took less notice of the sixteenth and seventeenth (or even the nineteenth and twentieth centuries); it looked forward rather to the twenty-first or perhaps even later centuries, to a world in the making out of elements largely conceived and brought to being outside what either Catholics or Protestants know as either Christendom or the Church. It was less concerned with what Luther, Calvin, Knox, or others on either side of divided Christendom's arguments might think, but with opening up dialogue in the name of the unique and undivided transcendent Christ with a generation for whom these names out of the past of Christian history are already meaningless and seem destined to become even more so. The thrust is now toward a force, that of secular or atheist humanism, which is presently intent on rejecting the whole script of the drama we were reading when the Council opened, its entire plot, all its *dramatis personae* and even its very author himself as irrelevant, unimportant, without existential meaning.

In a culture which has calmly heard the news that "God is dead" (has, in fact, read his obituary in the style of the New York *Times,* complete with the usual unctuous professions of bereavement from the White House), there is not likely long to be interest in Dr. Martin Luther's hypothetical stance vis-à-vis Vatican II nor, indeed, much speculation about how Leo X might react to the new murmurings from the non-monastic monks of the North and Northwest.

The Council's thrust is now fully focused on the *future* and on *dialogue* with the *present* and *coming* world of unbelief, dogmatic or practical. The evidences of this are in the new importance of the Secretariate for Dialogue with Atheist Humanism (as central to the work at the end of the Council as was that of the Secretariate for Christian Unity at the beginning), the content of the *Pastoral Constitution on the Church in the Modern World* (the last document to be worked in the Council), the significant polemic that it aroused within the Council, plus its invitation to a new dialogue in the future, the spirit and emphasis of the "messages to the world" proclaimed in the ceremonies of adjournment, and the "secular" pilgrimage of Pope Paul to the assembly of the United Nations, the Charter of which is still silent about God but eloquent with certain of the "validities" (basically Natural Law truths but always with close connection to the lessons of the Gospel) which must be the object of the "dialogue" of the indefinite future. It is this dialogue toward which the Council was pointed at its ending and which Pope Paul valiantly inaugurated at the United Nations by everything he said about peace and war, the sanctity of life, the irrationality of contraception in a truly loving and generous world, and the claims of "the Unknown God" upon a world eager for unity and disposed to study all ideas, values, and means essential to such unity.

And so, one sees the Council not at all in terms of *aggiornamento* merely understood as revising received values and ideas, least of all junking them, for the purposes of any merely present dialogue, however attractive or even urgent. But one sees it in terms of a setting of our house in order, balancing our own books, and discovering what friends and colleagues we may have kept or acquired for a future dialogue with a world presently indeed hostile, but which must also be encompassed by the Christian creed and code, beginning with basic friendship.

(In this connection, I am reminded that the dictionary sense of *aggiornamento* may include just such overtones of meaning as balancing one's books, not excluding the idea of deferred action pending such inventory of resources).

Moreover, against the background of this perspective of the Council one chooses a little more carefully the figures of speech, taken from the seasons of the year, by which one tries to express the function and the direction of the Council in God's plan for his people.

Some, I suspect, saw the Council as a season of harvest, an autumn after the long generations of hard polemic and divided struggle, a kind of coming together of the scattered workers to bring their different grapes to the wine-harvest (*vendemmia, vendage*) of the Lord.

One cannot see it so. Neither does one see the Council period as a golden summer of Christian history, glorious in its spiritual vitality, its religious action, its exploits for and in the Lord. Sober realism forbids such a reading either of the Church in our day or of the times which engulf us.

Pope John often used the figures of speech of spring. He was quoted by Mr. Norman Cousins (and others) as speaking of "opening the windows" as one does in spring and, especially, of seeking for the Church and her truth the verdant, pristine beauty that things have in spring. Perhaps this is closer to the mark, but it is not quite exact — yet.

Peasants have immemorially sought to anticipate the spring, to prepare for its beauty and even hasten it by planting grain that can mature (in the scriptural sense, even *die*, to come to life again) under the killing snows of the long winter. Pope John's Italian peasants speak proverbially of *il pane sotto il neve*, of how under the wintry snow there is life-giving bread so long as the seeds are maturing in preparation for the eventual spring.

One suspects that Pope John called the Council to provide just such a providential planting of certain *seed-ideas* against the severe winter of unbelief — of scientism, atheist humanism, and moral skepticism — which lies between us and the next springtime for both Christian faith and humane hopes, the spring that will add divine life and beauty to the valid human ideas and values which survive (may perhaps be strengthened by) a winter that he (in common with Newman and Soloviev, to name no others) saw fatally approaching.

Pope John thought of spring all the time; he talked of it readily and willingly. But he had served long years in two diplomatic centers, one in the East and one in the West, where the advance chill of the winter of unbelief (whether from jaded indifference, Marxist atheism, or existentialist negations) would have been felt deeply by so sensitive a spirit as his. Fortunately, his temperament and spirituality were formed in a part of the world and among a people who, with indomitable optimism, know how to plant before the winter the grain that survives the frosts and gives the spring at once its first beauty and its enduring life.

And if Pope John's prophetic preparation for the coming winter by so confident a late fall planting was providential for the Church (and, by the same token, for civilization itself), so must we see as dispositions of God's gracious purpose the capacity of Pope Paul for the disciplined, patient, and intelligent direction of God's Church through the severe initial period of the maturing of the Council's "seed-ideas."

For it is only as such "seed-ideas," for maturing in the dialogue persevering through a winter of unbelief which is destined to end in an eventual Second Spring, that the major actions and themes emerging from the Council experience take on something like the proportions due to the human good will engendered in the Council and the divine presence of the Holy Spirit. Thus understood, certain Council seed-ideas, whatever their present tentative and unformed shape, have manifest future potential for life and action in the coming spring. I suggest these as typical and as perhaps the most promising:

(1) the emphasis on the Church as the people of God (the new Israel, regenerating the world through a mystery); (2) the

concept of collegiality in its theological and, so to say, non-political dimensions; (3) the Catholic concept of the priesthood of the laity; (4) the pastoral and teaching functions of the liturgy (it is this emphasis that is new and probably explains the universal support of reform, even the vernacular, by the Council Fathers; most else was in *Mediator Dei*); (5) the emphasis on the person in an impersonal automated culture; (6) the communitarian nature of personality; (7) the Church as a universal sacrament of salvation; (8) the divine roots and measure of human life and love, a point of utter urgency for the survival of either and both in an age of test-tube and UNIVAC approaches to both life and love; (9) the recognition of a new humanism; (10) the condemnation of total war; (11) the suggestion of a world commission on justice and development; (12) the pattern in the Trinity for the Unity of the Church, God's only flock; (13) the relation to ecumenism of the Eucharist and of Peter; (14) the Church and the churches; (15) the missionary corollaries of collegiality, plus the "common good" of all the churches; (16) the mission of the laity in the temporal order and the validity of the goodness, truth and beauty served there; (17) the truth and holiness in non-Christian religions; (18) the real relation of the Crucifixion to Jew and Christian; (19) the *de facto* premise and nature of religious liberty, with the consequent demands on personal moral responsibility toward community and God of those who claim it so passionately.

That these seed-ideas finally found acceptance so unanimous in the Council argues more than the human ingenuity of bishops and their *periti*. And so, I conclude: the Spirit of God breathed where It willed in the Council. No person was more present, more active, more relevant in the Council's progress than the Third Person of the Trinity. That Divine Person was hard at work achieving His ancient task: *vivifying and unifying the Church* for a long, hard winter and *renewing the face of the earth* for a predestined spring. *Blessed be the Holy Spirit, the Paraclete!*

CHAPTER II

VATICAN II AND THE CHURCH IN THE MODERN WORLD

The Right Reverend Monsignor George G. Higgins

The Vatican Council's *Pastoral Constitution on the Church in the Modern World* is by far the longest of all the Conciliar documents and therefore extremely difficult to summarize briefly. I say this by way of indicating at the outset that it will be impossible for me to analyze the document in detail.

Since the fascinating history of the document has been recounted many times, it is not necessary here to provide a detailed account. On the other hand, it will be necessary to say at least a word about its history in order to put the document in context or perspective. The remote history of the *Constitution* goes back to the preparatory stages of the Council. You may recall that shortly after Pope John announced that he was going to convene a Council, all the bishops of the world were asked to send in suggestions for the agenda. These suggestions, when they were finally pulled together and correlated, totaled some eighteen or nineteen printed volumes. They are largely passè today. Reading them now, one is inclined to wonder whether the men who submitted them are the same men who voted in the Council. Be that as it may, the preparatory suggestions submitted by the bishops of the world did provide some useful background information and material for the preparatory commissions which were charged with the responsibility of drawing up a tentative agenda for the Council.

A number of bishops suggested that the Council deal with the Church and science, the problem of international social justice, the question of war and peace, racial discrimination, totalitarianism, etc. These suggestions were not acted upon immediately, but in 1962, just on the eve of the Council, Pope John delivered a major radio address in which he cited the need for a thorough re-examination of the inner life of the Church and added that the Council, at the same time, ought to address itself to the problems and the needs and the aspirations of the peoples of the world and specifically to such subjects as war and peace, freedom, international social justice, human brotherhood. In October, 1962, the Council, during the very early days of the first session, took heed of Pope John's recommendation and, as you will recall, issued a so-called message to mankind. This message did not get much publicity, possibly because it came out just at the time when the general public and the Fathers of the Council themselves were distracted by the election of new members to the Conciliar Commissions. In any event, the message did indicate that there was widespread agreement within the Council on the importance of saying something on the general subject of the Church in the modern world.

The proximate history of the *Constitution* goes back to the last week of the first session. The Council was badly bogged down at that time and still had no clear sense of direction. That is to say, no central theme had yet emerged from the rather general and somewhat disorganized discussions of the first few months. Be that as it may, on December 4, Cardinal Suenens, in a major address, called for a redrafting of the Schema *De Ecclesia*. He said that, just as Vatican I was the Council of papal primacy, Vatican II, in his judgment, should be the Council of the Church of Christ, the light of nations. He called attention specifically to the suggestions made by Pope John in his inaugural address — an address which will almost certainly go down as one of the most important documents of modern

Church history. Suenens proposed that, in the light of these suggestions, the doctrine on the Church should be approached in two distinct but related steps. First of all, the Council should look at the nature of the Church as the people of God and the Church's mission to preach the Gospel to all men. This, he said, would require a continuing dialogue between the Church and the world of today. Hence, he added, the Council would have to address itself to such problems as the dignity of the human person, the population problem, mass culture, and international social justice. The following day, as I recall, the then Cardinal Montini, in his first major address at the Council, enthusiastically seconded Cardinal Suenens' speech. I might add that many observers were of the opinion, rightly or wrongly, that Cardinal Montini was speaking, at least indirectly, for Pope John himself.

In January, 1963, shortly after the first session of the Council had adjourned, a mixed commission of some thirty members of the Theological Commission and thirty members of the Commission on the Lay Apostolate was charged with the responsibility of preparing the first draft of what we now know as the *Pastoral Constitution on the Church in the Modern World*.

I will not say any more about the history of the document except to add that it went through a very difficult period of incubation, understandably so in view of the fact that this was the first time that the subject of the Church in the modern world had been formally considered by an ecumenical council. In other words, the Commission had no precedent to go by.

A number of subcommission meetings were held in various cities in Europe, starting at Louvain, moving then to Zurich, then to Aricia, a suburb of Rome. There must have been eight or ten such meetings between January of 1963 and the end of the Council.

In passing, it will be appropriate to say a word about Louvain as the originial source of the document. Because of Cardinal Suenens' leadership, it was, in the beginning at least, almost exclusively a Louvain document. Subsequently, of course, experts from many other countries were brought into the picture. Louvain deserves an enormous amount of credit, not only for its contribution to the drafting of this particular *Constitution* but to many other Conciliar documents as well. It has been said more than once — and accurately, in my judgment — that this Council may well go down in history as the First Louvain Council, if only because such a large number of the more influential *periti* came from the Louvain tradition. Monsignor Philips, who was probably the most influential of all the *periti* in the Council, and was the man who steered *De Ecclesia* through and played an influential part in drafting the *Schema on the Church in the Modern World,* is a Louvain man. Canon Charles Moeller, who is now in Rome serving as the third man in the Congregation on the Doctrine of the Faith, is also from Louvain. A number of other Louvain professors whose names are less well known were also influential in the Council.

So much for the history of the document. Now let me say a brief word about its purpose and the audience to which it is directed.

It is important to note at the outset that the *Constitution* is specifically addressed to the whole of humanity, to all mankind. In this respect, it is similar to Pope John's encyclical *Pacem in Terris.* The decision to address the document to the whole of humanity obviously made for added difficulty in the choice of language, appeals to reason and Scripture, etc. In the end, however, I think the Commission met this challenge reasonably well. In this connection, I would call your attention to the marked contrast between the language and the style of this particular *Constitution* and the stilted and highly abstract style of so many earlier ecclesiastical documents.

The purpose of the *Constitution* was to indicate how the Council conceived of the purpose and the activity of the Church in the modern world. It was not meant to be a compendium of answers to specific problems facing the world, but rather a tentative or preliminary attempt to situate the Church in the modern world and to suggest new lines of thought which might, over a period of time, help the Church to think through a theology of the Church in the world.

It is important to bear in mind, in this connection, that it is a *pastoral* constitution. You know, of course, that there was a certain amount of disagreement among the Fathers as to whether it should be called a "constitution" at all. Some thought that this was too strong a word and that it would give too much authority to a document which of necessity had to be rather tentative in many of its conclusions. In the end, however, the Commission recommended that it be called a constitution but that the adjective "pastoral" be tacked on to indicate that it was not meant to be a dogmatic document solving problems in the field of dogmatic theology but rather that its emphasis was to be pastoral.

While the *Constitution* contains many new emphases, it is primarily a synthesis or bringing up-to-date of Catholic teaching. In other words, if I may repeat the point which I have already made, it was not meant to be a summary of moral theology, much less a compendium of answers to specific problems.

Now let me add a word about the methodology of the document. Bishop Mark McGrath served in the Council as the *Relator* on the *Introductio Expositiva* to the *Pastoral Constitution on the Church in the Modern World*. In this capacity, he was called upon to explain to the conciliar Fathers the methodology which had been employed in drafting the *Constitution*. Because of the very nature of the document, he pointed out, it was necessary that the real condition of today's world be described, at least in a general way, before any judgments were made about it. This inductive or descriptive methodology, he pointed out, was set forth in the *Introductio Expositiva* and was followed throughout the entire *Schema*. "Finally," he noted in concluding his *Relatio*, "the very newness of many of the questions proposed and their diversity . . . impose limits on our documents. General principles, either doctrinal or moral, are proposed, which principles frequently do not touch upon completely concrete solutions either because the problems involved require more mature examination, or because they must be considered by the faithful in a particular way in each region, under the guidance of their pastors."

The same point is made in the text of the *Constitution* itself:

Undeniably this Conciliar program is but a general one in several of its parts, and deliberately so, given the immense variety of situations and forms of human culture in the world. Indeed while it presents teaching already accepted in the Church, the program will have to be followed up and amplified since it sometimes deals with matters in a constant state of development. Still, we have relied on the word of God and the spirit of the Gospel. Hence we entertain the hope that many of our proposals will prove to be of substantial benefit to everyone, especially after they have been adapted to individual nations and mentalities by the faithful under the guidance of their pastors.

This preliminary word of caution with regard to the inherent limitations of the *Constitution* is applicable to each of its several chapters, but to none so much as Chapter III of Part II, which deals with economic and social life. In the very nature of things, this chapter deals with highly contingent matters which are in "a constant state of development: and consequently do not lend themselves readily to a univocal application of general principles, either doctrinal or moral." This will explain why the Council decided — wisely, in my opinion — to confine itself to the restatement of certain general principles and proposals which, hopefully, to repeat the words of the *Constitution,* "will prove to be of substantial benefit to everyone . . . after they have been adapted to individual nations and mentalities by the faithful under the guidance of their pastors."

The word "restatement" of principles is used here advisedly to suggest at the outset that this particular chapter of the *Constitution* does not pretend to break any new ground in the field of Catholic social teaching. For better or for worse, it is simply a brief restatement — or, if you will, a bringing up-to-date — of some, but by no means all, of the key principles and ideals outlined in papal pronouncements of the past seventy five years and, more specifically, in the two major encyclicals of Pope John XXIII, *Mater et Magistra* and *Pacem in Terris*. It is the Council's hope that Christians may be led by these ideals "and all mankind enlightened, as they search for answers to questions of such complexity."

The *Constitution's* explicit reference to the fact that mankind must search for answers to the complex questions of the modern world and that the Church wishes only to be of service to mankind in carrying out this search was echoed in Bishop McGrath's *Relatio* on the methodology of the document. "Thus," the Bishop stated, "the *Introductio Expositiva* ought to serve the purpose of our *Schema:* namely, to speak to the entire world, with a serious study of the problems which now concern its peoples, so that we may enter into a sincere dialogue with them, bringing forth the light of Christ for the solace, strength, peace, and more abundant life of all men in God."

The tone of the entire *Constitution*, then, derives from this purpose, namely, to enter into a dialogue with the modern world. In this respect, the document is closely modeled after the example set by John XXIII in his major encyclicals.

Mr. E. E. Y. Hales makes much of this point in his recent book entitled *Pope John and His Revolution*. "John," he writes in this perceptive study, "was as anxious as any previous pope to reaffirm some continuity in papal teaching; but in fact, in his brief reign, he changed both its spirit and its content. Still more surprising, he introduced a quite new note of hesitancy. He even hinted that he could be wrong, that he was only expressing his own view . . . [yet] doubt where doubt is due, as it is in all questions of politics and economics, is both intellectually proper and persuasively effective, and part of the charm of Pope John was his refusal to pontificate on public affairs; one feels that he is only giving advice; with Leo XIII and with Pius XI one is not allowed to forget that they are laying down the law."

To round out these introductory remarks about the methodology and the tone of the *Constitution,* I would call attention to still another similarity between the *Constitution* and John's encyclicals, namely, its spirit of Christian optimism. Again, what Mr. Hales says in this regard about John's pronouncements on contemporary social, economic, and political developments can also be said, *mutatis mutandis,* about the *Constitution:* "The note of alarm is scarcely audible."

Father Ernesto Balducci elaborates upon this point in his recent biographical study entitled *John — The Transitional Pope.* "Pope John's image of the Catholic of today," Balducci remarks, "is very different from that which was, for example, widely dominant in the era of his childhood, when the Catholic seemed to be more or less aware of being beseiged within a 'Christian world,' which was to be opposed and defended against a 'modern world.' . . ." As regards the modern world, Balducci continues,

> Pope John's Catholic does not feel himself alien to it; all that is good in it is his too. He desires and does what he can to promote the rights of the working classes; not only towards better social conditions but also towards full and direct political responsibility; he opposes clericalism in all its forms, including those in which capitalism seeks to perpetuate it, in disguise; he prefers the democratic system to any other political system, and this not simply as a make-shift . . . but because it best corresponds to the dignity of the human person; . . . he does not condemn the process of socialization brought about by improved techniques, but sees also its positive contributions, once it has been adequately incorporated and directed towards forms beneficial to the community as a whole; he does not reject the collaboration of other men who do not share his ideas, but seeks to work with them, within the limits permitted by real and proven good will. In short, Pope John's Catholic is perfectly at home in the modern world, and if he opposes it, he does so, not because he is a Catholic, but because the modern world is in many of its aspects inhuman, smitten asunder by the onslaught of evil; he opposes it because he is a man like his fellows, a man among men.

Balducci's portrait of Pope John's modern Catholic — a portrait
which, you will note, touches upon certain matters which lie
outside the formal scope of our discussion — can also serve as
a portrait of the Council's modern Catholic: one who is at
home in the modern world and seeks only to serve it and, more
specifically, to collaborate with other men of good will in
hastening the process of the unification of mankind, which, as
Balducci points out, "has shown an almost miraculous progress
in recent years."

Having said these things about the history, the purpose, and
the methodology of the document, I would now like to say a
few words about some of its recurrent themes and points of
emphasis.

In general, it seems to me that what the *Constitution* is
telling us is that we must learn, after the example of Pope
John, to be "all things to all men for the sake of Christ" and
must learn to be sympathetic toward everything in our native
culture which does not conflict with Christianity. We have not
been called to judge our own nation and our own culture, but
to help to save it — to help to save it from within, not by sterile
argumentation or snarling polemics, much less by force of numbers or by political tactics, but by the sheer force of Christian
charity and by our unselfish and totally disinterested involvement in the everyday work of the world.

It is no secret, of course, that we are sometimes accused of
shirking this commitment or disdaining this involvement. "The
great objection brought against Christianity in our time," a
priest-scholar of our own generation has observed, "and the
real source of the distrust which insulates entire blocks of humanity from the influence of the Church, has nothing to do with
historical or theological difficulties. It is the suspicion that our
religion makes its adherents inhuman" — in other words, that
it tends to isolate them from, instead of involving them in, the
common task of humanity, and causes them to lose interest in
the culture and the civilization of their own times.

Whether or not this criticism is justified, the providential example of good Pope John, who was the most beloved human being of this century, can serve to remind us that what the world expects from Christians and will instinctively honor and revere whenever it finds it, is the warmth of open-hearted and disinterested charity, a passionate concern for freedom, truth, and justice, and a profound sympathy for everything in modern culture and civilization which does not conflict with the Gospel.

We Catholics may find it difficult at first — more difficult perhaps than some of our non-Catholic contemporaries — to get used to the dialogue, for we have long been accustomed to think that on many, if not most, of the problems which we are now expected to discuss in "frank conversation" with our neighbors, we already have the answers. It may take us a while to realize that on all matters, except the essentials of our Faith, we have something to learn from the modern world — at least as much as we have to teach.

This is particularly true, I repeat, in the area of human freedom. "Our contemporaries," the Council points out, "make much of this freedom and pursue it eagerly, and rightly to be sure." The Council, as you might expect, warns against the danger of confusing true freedom with license, but true freedom, it insists, is a precious value and one which our contemporaries do well to pursue so eagerly "for only in freedom can man direct himself toward goodness."

From the doctrinal point of view, there is nothing new or original about the Council's statement on the importance of freedom in human society. Still and all, it has a new ring about it, possibly because Catholics in recent times have not always taken the lead in defending freedom as a civil right. The civil liberties movement in the United States, for example, has not had as much support from Catholics as one might have expected. The Council, with its historic *Declaration on Religious Freedom* and its frequent references to freedom in general, will undoubtedly help to correct this situation.

Please God, the Council will also help to bring about a greater measure of freedom within the Church itself. The Fathers have spoken out very forcefully on this subject. "In order that they may fulfill their function," we read at the end of the chapter on "The Proper Development of Culture," "let it be recognized that all of the faithful, whether clerics or laity, possess a lawful freedom of inquiry, freedom of thought, and of expressing their mind with humility and fortitude in those matters on which they enjoy competence."

In an effort to implement both the letter and the spirit of this declaration, a group of American Catholics have established an Institute for Freedom in the Church. It is arguable, I suppose, as to whether or not such an Institute is necessary or will serve any useful purpose. As I see it, however, the fact that so many intelligent, well-meaning laymen and priests think that it *is* necessary should give us pause and should lead us to take a good hard look at the problem of freedom within the Church. Unless and until we solve this problem, we are not likely to get very far in our dialogue with the modern world, which, to repeat the language of the *Constitution*, "rightly" attaches so much importance to freedom.

Up to this point I have been talking almost exclusively about the first section of the *Constitution*. This section deals with the more speculative aspects of the theology of the Church's role in the modern world. The second section deals with some of the practical problems of special urgency in the modern world — culture, politics, economic and social problems, the problem of war and peace and marriage and the family. For our purposes it will be necessary to limit ourselves to a very brief summary of the chapter on economic and social life.

First of all, the chapter on economic and social life, following the *Constitution*'s controlling methodology of starting inductively from the so-called "Signs of the Times," takes note at the very outset of what has come to be called "the revolution of rising expectations" — a phenomenon of which Barbara Ward has written about so extensively and to such good effect in recent years. In summary, the chapter points out that, while the economy of today is "an instrument capable of better meeting the intensified needs of the human family" . . . and while "the development of economic life could mitigate social inequalities (provided that it be guided and coordinated in a reasonable and human way), it is often made to embitter them, or, in some places, it even results in a decline of the social status of the underprivileged poor." The lack of balance between social classes, between various sectors of economic life, between particular regions of individual countries, and between rich and poor nations — these and other inequalities seriously jeopardize the peace of the world. "Our contemporaries," the document points out, "are coming to feel these inequalities with an ever-sharper awareness, since they are thoroughly convinced that the ampler technical and economic possibilities which the world of today enjoys can and should correct this unhappy state of affairs." According to this document, the basic cause of this unhappy state of affairs is the fact that "many people, especially in economically advanced countries, seem, as it were, to be ruled by economics, so that almost their entire personal and social life is permeated with a certain economic way of thinking. This is true both of nations that favor a collective economy and of others."

The legislative history of the *Constitution* makes it clear that this phrase "and of others," was meant to cover some of the leading capitalist nations of the world, including the United States, presumably. This double-barreled criticism of communist and capitalist nations will probably be resented by some Americans if the reaction to Père Lebret's recent book, *The Last Revolution*, is truly indicative of American sensitivity to such criticism. Père Lebret, of course, is much more explicit and much more pointed than the *Constitution* in his criticism of the Western powers. "There are many reasons," he writes, "for the reluctance of the more advanced and consequently richer peoples to take an objective view of the world situation. The main reason is a certain kind of greed, that is, an immoderate love of possessions. The former Colonial powers were often steeped in this vice, and never succeeded in freeing themselves from it. But the new major powers are possessed by the same vice in an even more virulent form."

Père Lebret's specific reference to the United States, which was almost brutally frank, has rubbed a number of Americans the wrong way. I happen to think that Lebret is too critical of the United States or, in any event, is much too doctrinaire in his critique of American capitalism. Be that as it may, Americans, in my judgment, would be well-advised to read his book with an open mind and, by the same token, would also be well-advised to ponder the significance of the fact that a Conciliar Commission made up of some sixty bishops representing every part of the world felt it necessary to say in the *Constitution on the Church in the Modern World* that "doctrines which obstruct necessary reforms," in economic life "under the guise of a false liberty" are no less erroneous than "those which subordinate the basic rights of individual persons and groups to the collective organization of production. . . ."

The reforms advocated by the *Constitution,* under the heading of Economic Development, are aimed at an "increase of the production of agricultural and industrial goods and of the rendering of service, for the purpose of making provision for the growth of population and of satisfying the increasing desires of the human race." Economic development, the document insists, "must remain under man's determination and must not be left to the judgment of a few men or groups possessing too much economic power or of the political community alone or of certain more powerful nations. It is necessary, on the contrary, that at every level the largest possible number of people and, when it is a question of international relations, all nations have an active share in directing that development."

In this connection, a special word of warning is addressed to those people in the economically underdeveloped areas of the world who hold back their unproductive resources or who deprive the community of the material or spiritual aid that it needs. They are told very pointedly that "they gravely endanger the common good." While they are never identified, I think it would be fair to say that perhaps a disproportionate percentage of them are to be found in certain traditionally Catholic countries, notably Latin America.

The section of the *Constitution* dealing with economic development is rounded off with a brief reference to the special problems of those workers who migrate from one country or district and contribute to the economic advancement of another nation or region. It would be safe to assume, I think, that this matter was included in the document at the request of bishops from the Mediterranean area who are understandably concerned about the plight of their own fellow citizens, who, in recent years, have migrated in such great numbers to Germany, Switzerland, England, and even to Ireland.

Finally, under the heading of Economic Development, we find a fleeting, two-sentence reference to automation. This once-over-lightly treatment of automation will come as a disappointment to those who expected the Council to "solve" the major problems confronting the modern world. Their feeling of disappointment is understandable, but they need to be reminded that it was not the purpose of the Council to "solve" specific problems but merely, as previously indicated, to enter into a sincere dialogue with mankind about some of these problems from the point of view of Christian principles and ideals.

The second section of the chapter on Economic and Social Life deals with certain principles concerning (1) the rights and duties of labor and (2) the subject of private property. It says nothing substantially new or original about either of these matters, but, in general, simply paraphrases the teaching of the social encyclicals, notably *Mater et Magistra*. The right of labor to organize and, under certain circumstances, to strike is restated as follows:

> Among the basic rights of the human person is to be numbered the right of freely founding unions for working people. These should be able truly to represent them and to contribute to the organizing of economic life in the right way. Included is the right of freely taking part in the activity of

these unions without risk of reprisal. Through this orderly participation joined to progressive economic and social formation, all will grow day by day in the awareness of their own function and responsibility, and thus they will be brought to feel that they are comrades in the whole task of economic development and in the attainment of the universal common good according to their capacities and aptitudes.

When, however, socioeconomic disputes arise, efforts must be made to come to a peaceful settlement. Although recourse must always be had first to a sincere dialogue between the parties, the strike, nevertheless, can remain even in present-day circumstances as a necessary, though ultimate, means for the defense of the workers' own rights and the fulfillment of their just desires. As soon as possible, however, ways should be sought to resume negotiations and discussions leading toward reconciliation.

The chapter on Economic and Social Life also favors the active sharing of all in the administration and profits of individual business enterprises, but it does not attempt to settle the old argument as to whether or not this is a requirement in strict justice. Significantly, however, it does make a further application, within the economic order, of the basic principle of participation in government by all members of a community or group. It says that "since more often, however, decisions concerning economic and social conditions, on which the future lot of workers and their children depends, are not made within the business itself but by institutions on a higher level, the workers themselves should have a share also in determining these conditions — in person or through freely elected delegates." This reference to workers being represented by "freely elected delegates" has meaning not only for the workers where there are no workers' organizations, but also for countries which have them but, like Spain, do not allow for a genuinely free election by the workers of their own representatives.

Private property is upheld in the document as "an extension of human freedom" and "one of the conditions for civil liberties," but the social nature of property and the common destination of earthly goods are stressed antecedently. As Father Donald

Campion, S.J., points out in his commentary on the *Constitution*, "the immediately relevant significance of this deliberate choice to reaffirm the earliest Christian tradition concerning property appears from a patristic citation made at this very point in the *Constitutions* 'Feed the man dying of hunger because if you have not fed him, you have killed him.' "*

Finally, the document, in three short sentences, also takes note of the fact that the forms of property ownership are varied today and are becoming increasingly diversified. These sentences were added to the final draft of the *Constitution* to meet the objections of those African and Asian bishops who had complained, with good reason, that earlier drafts were too Western or too European in tone and outlook and did not give due recognition to the various communitarian patterns of ownership which are found in their particular countries. Similarly, the document's concluding reference to the urgent need for land reform was inserted to take account of the situation in some of the economically underdeveloped areas of the world.

On balance, I think it must be said the *Constitution's* treatment of the problem of private ownership barely scratches the surface of an enormously complicated problem. The basic principles outlined in the document with regard to private ownership are valid as far as they go, but if they are to be of "substantial benefit to everyone," as the Council hopes they will have to be adapted "to individual nations and mentalities by the faithful, under the guidance of their pastors." Under the guidance of their pastors, yes — but, no less important, with the technical assistance of highly trained experts who, if I am not mistaken, are in short supply at this moment within the Catholic community, at least in the United States.

The chapter on Economic and Social Life closes with an appeal to Christians to play an active role in the field of social and economic reform. "Christians who take an active part in present-day, socioeconomic development and fight for justice and charity," the document reads, "should be convinced that

---

* In *The Documents of Vatican II* (New York: Guild, 1966), p. 192.

they can make a great contribution to the prosperity of mankind and to the peace of the world. In these activities let them, either as individuals or as members of groups, give a shining example. Having acquired the skills and experience which are absolutely necessary, they should observe the right order in their earthly activities in faithfulness to Christ and His Gospel. Thus their whole life, both individual and social, will be permeated with the spirit of the beatitudes, notably with a spirit of poverty.

"Whoever in obedience to Christ seeks first the kingdom of God, takes therefrom a stronger and purer love for helping all his brethren and for perfecting the work of justice under the inspiration of charity."

These concluding paragraphs of the chapter on Economic and Social Life recall an earlier reference to the same subject in the fourth chapter of the first section of the *Constitution* — a reference which reads in part, as follows: "The Christian who neglects his temporal duties neglects his duties towards his neighbor and even God, and jeopardizes his eternal salvation. Christians should rather rejoice that, following the example of Christ who worked as an artisan, they are free to exercise all their earthly activities by gathering their human, domestic, professional, social and technical enterprises into one vital synthesis with the religious values, under whose supreme direction all things are harmonized unto God's glory."

Whenever I read this section of the *Constitution on the Church in the Modern World,* I cannot help but recall the great Teilhard de Chardin's plaintive lament in his book, *The Divine Milieu,* about the tragic harm that has been done to so many good Christians by a truncated spirituality based on a false dichotomy between the spiritual and the temporal. "I do not think I am exaggerating," Chardin wrote almost a generation ago, "when I say that nine out of ten practicing Christians feel that man's work is always at the level of a 'spiritual encumbrance.' In spite of the practice of the right intentions, and the day offered every morning to God, the general run of the faithful dimly feel that time spent at the office or the studio, in the fields or in the factory, is time diverted from prayer and adoration. It is impossible not to work — that is taken for granted. But it is impossible, too, to aim at the deep religious life reserved for those who have the leisure to pray or preach all day long. A few moments of the day can be salvaged for God, yes, but the best hours are absorbed, or at any rate cheapened, by material cares. Under the sway of this feeling, large numbers of Catholics lead a double life or a crippled life in practice: they have to step out of their human dress so as to have faith in themselves as Christians — and inferior Christians at that."

In the spirit of the Council, then, we who are interested in Christian social action can make our own the advice which Chardin addressed to an earlier generation of committed Christians:

> Try, with God's help, to perceive the connection — even physical and natural — which binds your labour with the building of the Kingdom of Heaven; try to realize that heaven itself smiles upon you and through your works, draws you to itself; then, as you leave Church for the noisy streets, you will remain with only one feeling, that of continuing to immerse yourself in God. If your work is dull or exhausting, take refuge in the inexhaustible and becalming interest of progressing in the divine life. If your work enthrals you, then allow the spiritual impulse which matter communicates to you to enter into your taste for God whom you know better and desire more under the veil of His works. Never, at any time, 'whether eating or drinking,' consent to do anything without first of all realizing its significance and constructive value *in Christo Jesu,* and pursuing it with all your might. This is not simply a commonplace precept for salvation: it is the very path to sanctity for each man according to his state and calling . . . Right from the hands that knead the dough, to those that consecrate it, the great and universal Host should be prepared and handled in a spirit of adoration.

CHAPTER III

THE CHRISTIAN COMMITMENT IN THE MODERN WORLD

F. X. Murphy, C.SS.R.

From a strictly statistical viewpoint, it can hardly be maintained that the Catholic Church or Christianity itself is a great success in the contemporary world. After 1900 years of missionary activity, it embraces but one-sixth of the world's population; and, on a graduated guess, I dare say that this percentage represents the fullest extent of the Church's expansion even all through the medieval period. In the light of Christ's commission to preach the gospel to every nation and to every creature, the achievement has long been in need of a profound reassessment.

The task of rethinking its own inner nature, and of assessing its operational genus, has been broached by Vatican Council II; and general lines for an updating or *aggiornamento* have been hammered out and accepted by the vast majority of conciliar prelates. As a consequence, the obligation incumbent upon the people of God — both laity and clergy — now is to draw out the implications of the Council's revolution, and to make haste to do something drastic about them.

I use the word *drastic* deliberately; for I am convinced that the time-scale in which we are now operating does not afford the Church the luxury of taking its time — in the older expression, of viewing things almost exclusively *sub respectu aeternitatis.* I would like to make it immediately clear, however, that contrary to older ways of considering things, this demand for rapid change, for new methods, and even for a substantial turnabout in certain fields, does not imply a repudiation of the past. The use of the very word *change* should not be taken to mean that what went before was erroneous or wrong. I believe that a good part of the resistance to the conciliar decisions comes from the fear that in accepting new perspectives, in viewing some of our dogmatic positions and moral convictions from a different vantage point, it will be necessary to condemn as wrong or to negate what was held or taught yesterday. This is a temptation brought about by a too facile application of logic and the categories of Aristotelian criteriology to the world of spiritual and human reality. Logic and its rules are useful, indeed necessary even in theology and the social sciences; but no system of thinking or technique should be allowed to dominate spheres of experience and reflection to such a degree that it prevents true progress. More particularly in the realm of the spirit, where a breakthrough into a totally new manner of conceiving a science or art is possible, traditional truths, even in the religious sphere, must be constantly subjected to restatement if not re-evaluation. Actually, of course, familiarity with the zigzagging history of dogma or moral theology from the second to the sixteenth centuries renders this observation superfluous. Today, the pattern for changeover in our current theology has been actually set by the revolutions experienced in the physical sciences over the past hundred years from biology and medicine to psychiatry and nuclear physics. Religion and theology should not be stepchildren in this regard.

There is no question here of repudiating divine revelation or the facts of the Christian experience thus far. These are actually the data upon which the renewed Christian approach is to base its stance. Where the theological changeabout commences, however, is in the attention paid to man as he is in himself, living in the twentieth century. Christian theology in the past was directed much more to the evaluation of divine revelation almost in a

vacuum; it began and ended with a very philosophic and therefore very limited concept of eternity hanging between the two
poles of creation and the parousia; and particularly through consideration of such teaching as predestination, it tended to consider man as a sort of unfortunate appendage almost lost within
the perspective of salvation history.

While the perspective of salvation history is now being high-
lighted, Vatican Council II has seen fit to focus its attention much
more designedly on the object of divine revelation — on man,
who is at once the reason for God's interest in the world, and
the most important link between the two poles of eternity. This
is not to suggest that the twentieth century has become a sort
of halfway mark in the development of that sacred history; that
point was definitely reached at the moment of the Incarnation.
But this decade of the twentieth century is a sort of halfway
notch; it is certainly a decisive moment in that history. It marks
a turning point, every bit as eventful as the Constantinian experi-
ment of the fourth century, or the Italian renaissance that had
its roots in the fourteenth century.

A turning point in the christianization of our contemporary
world — and by this I do not refer merely to the conversions of
millions of hitherto unbaptized individuals — should have been
achieved by Vatican II. What I mean is that, as a result of the
Council, Christians generally should feel that they have been
given a new commission so to penetrate the consciousness of
modern man that, in Pope John's expression, they will drive
through to the consciences of our contemporaries, in all climes
and spheres of existence. The Council happened in time to turn
the tide that seemed as though it were drifting toward a post-
Christian and, therefore, thoroughly godless civilization. The
Council has given a revolutionary twist to the direction of
modern religious thought; it can have supplied the impetus
needed for the reconstitution of a new Christian culture.

A sign of the substantial achievement in that revolutionary
redirection was given by Pope Paul's appearance before the
United Nations Assembly in New York. There he was able to

state that his presence in addressing that body was the first
time a representative of the Christian religion has ever truly
come face to face with the nations of the world. This claim was
not challenged or contradicted by leaders of other Christian
churches; nor was it repudiated by the professedly atheistic or
non-Christian nations. The ferment of the Council, thus high-
lighted, has been absorbed by many of the movements among
other Christian bodies that preceded the Council, some of which,
such as the ecumenical efforts of the World Council of Churches,
had a definite influence on the thinking and decision of the
Council itself. It has likewise been the stimulant to a great wave
of interest, and to a considerable stirring within strictly Catholic quarters. The extent and the possibilities of this movement
insofar as it means a full-scale commitment to the problems of
our contemporary world are the themes I am most interested in
developing here.

If I may be permitted a slight aside that does, however, have
a bearing on our topic, I might remark that a number of theologians and journalists had been hoping that Pope Paul would do
something of a truly revolutionary character to, shall we say,
start the ball rolling with a bang in regard to reorganization in
the Church's curial offices, and possibly likewise in its educational organizations. But it is now evident that the present Holy
Father is very conscious of his function as the conserver of
tradition as well as the recipient of charismata of change. Taking occasional notice of his critics who feel that he does not want
to move quickly enough, the Pope has replied that after all he
is the Pope; and that, as the head of the Church, he should have
a right to call the plays in accord with his own timing. No one can
fault him here. What is undeniable on this score is that Pope
Paul is determined on change, and on radical rearrangements.
His pacing will probably prove the most successful in the long
run; but for those of us involved in the immediate sprinting, his
deliberate gradualism seems at times almost to be giving aid and
comfort to the enemy. There are those among us who would
prefer a faster pace and a more positive insistence on the con-

ciliar directives — an ordering of the old guard into line quickly. For we fear that the time-scale of history is set at a much faster pace than the Vatican realizes. Tomorrow alone will tell whose prognosis was closest to reality. Meanwhile, it is hopeful to know that the Pope is just as set on change as his most rabid subjects.

To draw these observations into practical focus, it may be helpful to relate them to experience. I have just returned from a much too rapid trip that took me around the periphery of the great African continent. The first of my observations is the fact that while, generally speaking, the Catholic Church tends to view Africa as a highly diversified totality, in terms of a mission territory, in actuality the Church is solidly founded in almost all the African nations, and exhibits both the similarities and the differences to be found in other conglomerations of nation-based churches. The missionary activities over roughly the last hundred years have been eminently successful in laying deep and solid foundations, so that you have Congolese Catholics, Kenyan, South African, Senegalese, and Nigerian Christians, to mention but a few, who feel that they have their own Christian traditions and that they are every bit as solidly members of Christ's Mystical Body as are the Irish, Italian, German, or American Catholics of our more immediate acquaintance.

Time-wise, their churches are comparatively new; but family-wise, they possess strong Christian roots; and institution-wise, though many of their priests and bishops are still foreigners — or expatriates, as I have been taught more recently to refer to them — these very bishops and priests quickly discover that there are attitudes and traditions in these countries, among the older Catholics and Christians, that enjoy the very same pride of place that parallel Christian traditions enjoyed in their own country of origin.

Now what is eminently characteristic of this missionary Church is the fact that from the very start, the missionaries, the catechists, and the converts were committed to their immediate world. They dealt with problems thrown up by older forms of tribal or national worship. They concerned themselves with the organization of education; with the introduction of hygienic and medicinal practices hitherto unknown to these peoples; and to a great extent, they influenced political policies even though almost invariably these were the colonial policies of the parent government. Whatever may have been the success of these missionaries and their earlier converts, they simply could not and did not avoid a deep commitment to the things of their world; and the witness they gave to the presence of Christ in the Church had an immediate bearing on the family, on the cultural, socioeconomic, and political outlook of their own people and those about them.

It is the height of absurdity therefore for the post-Conciliar expert in missiology of Christian social or political action to tell the bishops and leaders of these churches that what they have done or are doing is all wrong and that they must consequently introduce radical changes in their missionary attitudes and technical achievements. The latter turnabout may be necessary, but it cannot and must not be introduced as an immediate repudiation of all that went before, particularly when you have strongly established churches witnessing to the fact that earlier mission activities were successful. What is unfortunate is that there have been recently a small number of so-called experts in missiology on the new cavalier theology who have traveled through these areas preaching radical change, and the result has been close to disastrous; for it has further convinced a number of bishops and seminary directors that almost any liberal interpretation of the Council's documents is explosively dangerous, and that perhaps the whole Council, except for a few minor liturgical changes, was not truly relevant to their missionary territories.

Actually, change is needed in the effort further to christianize these countries; but it is the very same type of change that is necessary in Washington, or in New York, Chicago, or Rome itself. Proportionally now, most of these new nations of Africa have a number of Christians equivalent to the numbers of Christians in many European and American lands. What is more, the influence they have had as Christians on the newly formed governments is for the most part on a parallel with that exercised by Christianity in our European and American governments. Thus the burden for the actualization of Christianity in our world is to be shared almost equally by these nations along with the older so-called Christian peoples.

In pursuing the problem of the concrete effort to be made in Christianizing our civilization in accord with the prescriptions of the *Pastoral Constitution on the Church in the Modern World*, it should not be necessary to outline once more the content of that document. For it is a Christian Manifesto whose observations and directives should by now have seeped into the consciousness of every articulate Catholic; and whose spirit should be breathed upon the vast sea of Christians who daily call upon Almighty God to "send forth His spirit and renew the face of the earth."

Part of my objection to outlining the contents of what used to be called *Schema 13* is the fact that what is all too frequently outlined is seldom studied or absorbed in its totality. Similarly, I feel conscious of a great danger that in the interests of conservatism, while we outline, this document will be subjected to a tough type of legalistic exegesis; and we will discover that its dynamic drive is being short-circuited by the static type of metaphysical analysis that has greatly hampered the Church in its dealing with the contemporary world over the last four centuries. It was, of course, this very domination of a fearful and deadening tradition that the Council and this document in particular attempted, and succeeded in destroying. Unfortunately, documents and directives do not destroy mentalities.

I believe that the mind of the Church right now is focused on action, and upon the type of theological and theoretical preparation that can guide and safeguard the integrally spiritual creativity of that action. As indicated by Pope Paul and the bishops at the moment of promulgation, and in frequent papal exhortations since the close of the Council, this document is to be taken as a platform of achievement. Its doctrines and teaching represent a level of commitment that should be accepted and absorbed as the Church's stand here and now. The sentences and paragraphs should be read and understood as they read — *prout sonant* — thus giving the Holy Spirit a chance to speak out over the din of past prejudices, and over against previously determined stances.

Viewed in this fashion, it will quickly be seen that the *Pastoral Constitution*, although actually composed by way of a series of compromises, and although occasionally seeming to embody apparent contradictions, is really a well-integrated challenge that expresses a religious commitment in, to, and for the world. It must be obvious to all but the most intransigent dogmatician that, at the Pope's request, a supreme effort was made by the Council Fathers not to define but to describe man in his human condition, and that this has been achieved with incredible realism all through the first part of the document.

Incidently, it was this magnificent achievement that Pope Paul made use of in his closing discourse on December 7, when in summing up the work of the Council he said explicitly that the most important feature was its concentration on man — since it is truly man who is the most important object in creation, and it is really only through man that men can arrive at God.

Thus the whole Council in concentrating on man as epitomized in the People of God, with its total focus on man's present condition, has brought about, or should have a substantial change in the direction of the Church's consideration of itself and of its place in our world.

That there should be a problem of conscience concerning the presence of the Christian in the world has always caused me some confusion. It strikes me as absurd that there are men who have accepted the office of successors to the apostles as bishops, and of other Christs as priests, and who yet feel that direct contact with the world, an inmixing with contemporary men and women, presents great danger to their faith, and opens paths to perversion as far as their spiritual values and practices are concerned. In particular, it seems to me that the fearful cry of "secularism" brought against contemporary society is a terrible admission of defeat and inadequacy on the part of such Christian leaders. It means that their witness to Christ in the world has failed and, whereas they had attempted to convince modern man that he should have faith in God, they have merely convinced him that he must have faith in himself, since the apparent faith of so many Christian leaders was inadequate spiritually, and so unsatisfactory in the realm of charity and philanthropy.

By way of conclusion, I would merely like to insist that the primary requirement of the Church dealing with today's world is to restore the reputation enjoyed by the primitive disciples: "Look how these Christians love one another." This means that the men behind the institutional Church must now put their minds and energies to creating an image of the bishop, priest, and religious as one who actually imitates Christ "by having compassion on the multitude." This means likewise that the whole people of God will be conscious of their obligation to reduce to practice the doctrines and directives of the *Pastoral Constitution*, considering themselves also as the servants of the servants of God.

CHAPTER IV

THE ISSUE OF CHURCH AND STATE
AT VATICAN COUNCIL II

John Courtney Murray, S.J. *

No formal document on the relations between Church and state issued from Vatican Council II, although the issue had appeared in the legislative history of the Council. The original schema of the Constitution on the Church, distributed on November 10, 1962, contained a chapter (9) "On the Relations of Church and State." It was a revision of a prior text, also written by the Theological Commission, "On the Relations of Church and State and on Civil Tolerance." Also during the preconciliar period — in December, 1960 — a schema on religious freedom was prepared by a subcommission of the Secretariat for Promoting Christian Unity, meeting in Fribourg. It was recognized that the particular issue of religious freedom needed to be clarified, if there was to be any hope of instituting proper ecumenical relationships between the Catholic Church and the other Christian churches and communities.

In June, 1962, Cardinal Bea presented to the Central Commission a revision of the Fribourg schema, containing three brief chapters, the third of which was entitled "On the Relations between the Church and Civil Society." At the same time the

---

* Reprinted with permission from the December, 1966 issue of *Theological Studies*.

Theological Commission presented its own schema — the first of the two mentioned above. A lengthy discussion of the two schemata proved inconclusive; their respective tendencies were quite diverse. The matter was referred to Pope John XXIII, who created in July, 1962, a mixed committee whose function would be to effect a reconciliation of the two tendencies. (In the end, this committee — composed of Cardinals Ciriaci, Ottaviani, and Bea, Msgr. Willebrands, and Fr. Tromp — never met.) In that same month the Secretariat schema was revised, to take account of certain views expressed in the schema of the Theological Commission. In February, 1963, the Secretariat decided further to revise its schema and to leave aside the Church-state issue. This new revision, approved by the Secretariat in May, 1963, was presented to the Coordinating Commission in July, and the decision was reached that it should be Chapter 5 of the schema on ecumenism to be presented by the Secretariat. (The details of the long delay in getting the text printed need not concern us here.) Chapter 9 was omitted from the revised schema on the Church. And thus it came about that only the issue of religious freedom was discussed by the Council.

The explicit intention of the Declaration on Religious Freedom was narrowly defined in the final text, namely, "to develop the doctrine of recent popes on the inviolable rights of the human person and on the constitutional order of society" (n. 1).* Nevertheless, in the course of fulfilling this relatively restricted doctrinal intention, the Declaration made certain significant contributions towards a development of doctrine in regard to the Church-state issue. In its turn, the *Constitution on the Church in the World Today* confirmed, and in certain respects advanced, this development. The purpose of this article is to analyze the development.

THE NEW PROBLEMATIC

In general, the development consisted in a transformation of the state of the question. A movement in a new direction had

---

* N. refers to paragraph number in *The Declaration*.

already been begun by Leo XIII. From early Christian times, through the medieval era, through the later era of the French classical monarchy, and through the post-Reformation epoch of confessional absolutism, the primary issue had been stated in terms of the relationship between the two powers, spiritual and temporal — pope and emperor, pope and king or prince. This issue retained a mode of its validity for Leo XIII. He did not indeed contend for "union of Church and state" on the model of the *ancien régime,* wherein the Union of Throne and Altar entailed an enclosure of the national Church within the national kingdom and some consequent manner of subordination of Church to state. However, against the dogma of "separation of Church and state" in the sense of Continental laicism, he consistently argued for an orderly relationship between ecclesiastical and political authority. At the same time he transformed this ancient issue of the dyarchy by including it within a broader statement of the question, to which the conditions of the time — the progressive laicization and also industrialization of society in Continental Europe — led him.

The new terms were the "Church," both as a spiritual authority and also as the community of the Christian faithful, and "human society" in the whole range of its institutional life — social, economic, and cultural, as well as political. Within this broader context, the issue of the dyarchy tended to appear, less as a formally juridical issue of structural relationships between the two powers, than as the wider issue of their reciprocal cooperation toward the integral good of the "same one man, both Christian and citizen," whom they both encounter — and thus encounter each other — in the concrete life of society. What supremely mattered to Leo XIII was the establishment of a Christian order in the whole of society. The orderly relationship between the two powers was simply a subordinate aspect of this larger goal. The issue of the dyarchy as such had begun to lose its ancient primacy.

Vatican Council II pursued and prolonged this line of development. The chief witness here is the whole *Constitution on the*

Church in the World Today. Of particular significance are Part 1, Chapter 3, "On Human Activity in the Whole World," and Chapter 4, "On the Function of the Church in the World Today." The basically Leonine inspiration of these two chapters is instantly visible; but so too is the development of doctrine beyond its Leonine stage. And again the source of the development lies in a broadening of the perspectives in which the question is viewed.

For Leo XIII, "human society" meant concretely the Europe of the nineteenth century. His religious interests did indeed range much farther afield. But the focus of his political and social teaching, as of his diplomacy, was obviously on the European nations, chiefly the so-called Catholic nations, as these underwent the shattering impact of the French Revolution, Continental laicism, and the Industrial Revolution. In contrast, for Vatican II, "human society" meant quite literally the whole world —and the whole world as it is everywhere undergoing the more shattering impact of the technological revolution of the twentieth century.

Again, both Leo XIII and Vatican II were concerned with religion as the basic dynamic element — both salvific and civilizational — in the life of the world, whether in the broader or in the narrower sense of the term "world." For Leo XIII, however, religion uniformly meant Christianity and Christianity uniformly meant the Catholic Church, which he conceived to be not only the unique but also the exclusive ecclesial form of Christianity. The Christian religion in this Catholic sense was for him the "teacher and nurse of Christian civilization," that is, the civilization of Europe. (He also firmly supported the religio-political privileges of France with regard to missionary activity in the East and Far East, which dated from the days of Francis I, and which resulted, in effect, in the identification of Catholic expansion and the expansion of French national culture — a result not altogether happy in its confusion of Christianization and Europeanization.) In particular, the Christian religion in its Catholic sense was, for Leo XIII, the origin and support of the unity of the Catholic European peoples. Insofar as he paid attention to the religion and to the ecclesial communities which emerged from the Reformation, it was to regard them as representing, not only religious error, but also a solvent of traditional European culture. (Be it noted, on the other hand, that he was the first Pope to use the phrase "separated brethren."[1])

In this sense his religio-civilization outlook was related to his historical outlook, which was simple and narrow. The key to it is in the famous once-upon-a-time passage ("Fuit aliquando tempus . . .") in *Immortale Dei*.[2] The medieval era was the golden age of Christian unity, of harmony between the two powers, and of the obedience of princes and peoples to the authority of the Church. Then came the Reformation, which was a revolt against the authority of the Church, the rupture of Christian unity, and the origin of profound civilizational change. Later, by virtue of logical as well as historical sequence, came the Revolution, which was a revolt against the sovereignity of God Himself, a schism within the Catholic nations, a disruption of the relationship between the two powers, and the beginnings of the laicization of European culture. Within these historical perspectives, whose focus of origin was in the past, Leo XIII could not but call for a return to a Christian unity once possessed, to an ecclesiastical obedience once rendered, to the matrix of a culture once fertile of Christian forms.

Vatican II, however, relinquished this retrospective view of history and adopted a prospective view. Its perspectives open out from the present. They are set by the signs of the times, which are chiefly two. The first is a rising consciousness of the dignity of the human person; correlative with it is a mounting movement toward the unity of the human family. Therefore the problem for the Church, as for man himself, is an increasing realization, in all manner of institutional forms, both of human

---

[1] Lettre à Mgr. Satolli à propos du Congrès des Religions, 8 Septembre 1895 (*Lettres Apostoliques de S. S. Léon XIII, Texte latin avec la traduction française en regard* [Paris: Maison de la Bonne Presse, n.d.] 257). This edition is hereafter cited as "Bonne Presse," with volume and page.

[2] Bonne Presse 2, 32.

dignity and of human unity. "As we undertake our work therefore," said the Council in its Message to Humanity on October
20, 1962, "we would emphasize whatever concerns the dignity
of man, whatever contributes to a genuine community of
peoples." Hence the work of the Church, as the work of man
himself, looks to the future. It implies a movement forward —
not a return but a renewal.

Moreover, the doctrinal perspectives of Vatican II are ecumenical, whereas Leo XIII's were not. Not only did the Council
gratefully acknowledge the "heritage of faith handed down by
the apostles" as found in the Eastern Churches, and the Christian and ecclesial elements retained in the separated churches
and ecclesial communities in the West, and the religious values
in non-Christian religions, and in particular the community of
tradition between Christianity and Judaism. In the same spirit
it also recognized that the future of civilization on this earth
depends, not solely on the Church, but on the widest possible
co-operative effort. The Council reiterated the Leonine position,
as in this text from the *Constitution on the Church in the World
Today:* "The Church believes that she, through each of her
members and through the entirety of her community, can contribute greatly toward making the family of men and its history
more human" (n. 40). But there is a new development: "In
addition, the Church gladly sets a high value on the contributions which other Christian churches and ecclesial communities
have made and are making, in a united effort, toward the fulfilment of the same task" (*loc. cit.*). Leo XIII never said that.
Nor did he rise to the humility of the further statement: "At the
same time, [the Church] holds firmly that she can be assisted to
a great extent and in a variety of ways by the world itself, by
individual men and by human society, through their endow-
ments and efforts, in preparing the way for the gospel" (*loc. cit.*).

Continuity, however, is here visible. Leo XIII took the first
decisive step toward healing the breach between the Church and
the European world of his day, which had been his unhappy
legacy from the pontificate of Pius IX. He offered to this limited

"world" the assistance of the Church for the healing of the ills of the time. Vatican II took a much longer step in the same direction. It repeated Leo's offer — on a more generous scale — and thus reaffirmed an ancient tradition. It also did something new. In its turn it asked the world — conceived in all its global sweep and growing complexity — for its own assistance, not merely for the healing of the ills of the times (upon which, in the spirit of John XXIII, the Council did not lengthily dwell), but more importantly for the fulfillment of the signs of the times. The Council repeatedly insisted that the inherent sense of the gospel summons the Church to the task of lifting man to his true dignity and of knitting the bonds of human community. It also insisted that the world must know itself to be summoned to the same task by the stirrings within its own consciousness.

It is not the intention of this essay to pursue in detail, or to estimate the adequacy of, the Council's solution to its own developed version of the Leonine problematic. The first point here is the new conception of the problematic. Its terms are not now, as they were for Leo XIII, the Catholic Church and human society in Europe. The terms are wider — religion in its full ecumenical sense and human society throughout the wide world. The second point is that, again in continuity with Leo XIII, the Council situated the narrow issue of Church and state within the context of its own widened problematic. Thus it effected a further transformation of the state of the narrower question. And in consequence it opened the way to a development of doctrine on the matter. It can hardly be said that the Council itself wrought out the development. Nevertheless, it offered certain guidelines. They may be gathered both from the *Declaration on Religious Freedom* and from the *Constitution on the Church in the World Today*.

DIGNITATIS HUMANAE

In the first place, in accordance with the worldwide outlook of the Council, the Declaration acknowledges the fact of the religiously pluralist society as the necessary historical context of the whole discussion. The acknowledgment is implicit in the intention of the document to deal with a universal human right. It becomes more explicit in the section on corporate religious freedom (n. 4) and in the concluding pastoral exhortation (nn. 14–15). Leo XIII, in contrast, by reason of his restricted and retrospective view of history, had tended to assume, as the historical premise of the Church-state question, the religious unity of the Catholic nations, so-called, and the historic rights acquired by the Church within this limited geographical context. His thought was still, in a sense, tributary to the view developed largely in the post-Reformation era and accepted then by both Catholic and Protestant rulers and by their respective churches, that the introduction of religious pluralism into a religiously unitary society was illegitimate; that it was to be resisted by the power of government; that government could do no more than tolerate it, and then only when religious dissent had so established itself as a social force that the attempt to eradicate it by force would do more harm than good.

In the second place, the Declaration embraces the political doctrine of Pius XII on the juridicial state (as it is called in Continental idiom), that is, on government as constitutional and as limited in function — its primary function being juridicial, namely, the protection and promotion of the rights of man and the facilitation of the performance of man's native duties. The primacy of this function is based on Pius XII's personalist conception of society — on the premise that the "human person is the foundation, the goal, and the bearer of the whole social process,"[3] including the process of government. In contrast, Leo XIII had held a more statist and moralist view of society. In his classic encyclicals, up to *Rerum novarum*, the traditional distinction between society and state is obscured; the foundation and bearer of the social process is the ruler (or, if you will, the state); and the goal of the ruler-state is the common good considered as an ensemble of virtues in the body politic, notably

---

[3] Cited by John XXIII in *Pacem in Terris* (AAS 55 [1963] 263) from Pius XII's Radio Message, Christmas, 1944.

the virtue of obedience to rule. It is not until *Rerum novarum* that the dignity of the human person and the inviolability of his rights begins to emerge as determinant of social and political doctrine, thus affording the point of departure for the doctrine of Pius XII, John XXIII, and the Council.

In the present matter, the significance of the political doctrine of the Declaration (as also of the *Constitution on the Church in the World Today*) lies in its disavowal of the long-standing view of government as sacral in function, that is, as invested with the function of defending and promoting religious truth as such. This view of government is visible even in Leo XIII. Its disavowal by the Declaration follows on its intention to develop the doctrine of more recent popes on the constitutional order of society. In this development the function of government appears as the protection and promotion, not of religious truth, but of religious freedom as a functional right of the human person. This is a secular function, since freedom in society — notably religious freedom — is a secular value, as are the values of justice and love or civic friendship. All three of these values are rooted in the truth about the human person, which is the truth upon which the whole social and political order rests. Hence the tutelage of these values is proper to the notion of government as secular in the full range of its purposes. It is true that the final text of the Declaration is inadequate in its treatment of the limitations imposed on government by sound political doctrine. Nevertheless, the disavowal of the old notion of government as sacral in function is sufficiently clear, both from the firm statement of the essential juridical function of government (n. 6), and also from the earlier statement that the proper purpose of government is to have a care for the common temporal good and that it would exceed its limits were it to presume to direct or impede religious acts (n. 3). These statements, jejune though they are, exclude the notion that government is to be the judge of religious truth, the defender of the true faith, or the guardian of religious unity.

In the third place, in systematic harmony with its own doctrine on the universal right to religious freedom and on the limitations of governmental power in matters religious, the Declaration makes the statement: "The freedom of the Church is the fundamental principle in what concerns the relations between the Church and governments and the whole civil order" (n. 13). The import of this statement is considerable. It opens the way to a new structure of Catholic doctrine on Church and state — to a renewal of the tradition whose great exponent was Gregory VII: "In moments of considered solemnity, when their tone was passionate and their religious feeling at its deepest, Gregory VII and his contemporaries called the object toward which they were striving the 'freedom of the Church.'"[4] In modern times Leo XIII powerfully effected a renewal of the Gregorian tradition: "A major significance of Leo XIII in the history of doctrinal development lies in his great effort to rescue the Church from the regalist tradition — from that servitude to the state under which it had lain for nearly half a millenium of regalism. The servitude dated from the triumph of Philip the Fair's lawyers over Boniface VIII, which had been solidified by the rising centralized monarchies, especially in France. In a full view, Leo XIII appears as the Gregory VII of the nineteenth century, returning under the stress of the times [as regalism reappeared in laicist garb] to the splendid device under which the great Hildebrand fought his battle, 'the freedom of the Church.'"[5] The phrase occurs in well over a hundred texts in the Leonine corpus, of which perhaps one fourth have to do with the Roman question. One providential result of this tragic impasse was that it drew the attention of the papacy to the "fundamental principle."

The implications of the principle were not worked out in the post-Leonine canonist systematizations. Oddly enough, the inarticulate major premise controlling these systematizations

[4] G. Tellenbach, *Church, State and Christian Society at the Time of the Investiture Contest* (tr. R. F. Bennett; Oxford: Blackwell, 1940) p. 126.

[5] John Courtney Murray, S.J., "Leo XIII: Separation of Church and State," *Theological Studies* 14 (1953) 192.

seems to have been the civilist formula, the "unity of the Church." In the late medieval view of the civilists the formula stressed the role of the prince in the construction of the *ecclesia*, that is, *christianitas*, the Christian world. The role of the prince, now understood as the "Catholic state," in the construction of the Christian society, now contracted to the dimensions of the "Catholic nation," seems likewise to have been a major preoccupation of the modern canonists. The text of *Dignitatis humanae*, however, made vital contact with the profound doctrine of Leo XIII, and thus with the genuine tradition.

After the vote on the fifth conciliar schema (*textus recognitus*, which was presented on October 25, 1965), an amendment was submitted by three Fathers, suggesting that in n. 13 the text should read "fundamental condition" instead of "fundamental principle," in referring to the freedom of the Church. The reasons for the change were not given. At any rate, the substitute text would have been in harmony with the received opinion in the canonist school, according to which the freedom of the Church is merely the fundamental condition of right relationships between Church and state, whereas the fundamental principle is the Church's exclusive right to a situation of legal privilege. The amendment was rejected. The laconic reason advanced by the Secretariat read: "It is a question of a true principle." The response was not wholly adequate.

The text of the schema was, in fact, an implicit citation from the Encyclical Letter of Leo XIII to the French Cardinals, *Notre consolation* (May 3, 1892). In it he defends himself against the charge that his policy of *ralliement* in France was inconsistent with the policy of opposition that he was adopting toward the government of Italy — the former policy being religious in inspiration; the latter, political. The policies, he replies, are profoundly consistent, since "the question which concerns us in Italy is also eminently religious in as much as it is related to the fundamental principle of the freedom of the Church,"[6]

---

[6] Lettre encyclique aux Cardinaux Français, 3 mai 1892 (Bonne Presse 3, 127).

which was also the principle at stake in France. The freedom of the Church is not merely a true principle; it is the fundamental principle governing the relations of the Church with all governments.

This is not the place to explain in detail what the formula "the freedom of the Church" meant to Gregory VII within the context of medieval Christendom. The Vatican Declaration, however, gives an adequate explanation of what the freedom of the Church concretely means today. In an implicit citation from Pius XII it is said to mean "that stable condition of right and of fact [which guarantees] the necessary independence [of the Church] in the fulfilment of her divine mission" (n. 13). Moreover, a proper distinction is made between the Church as an authority and as a community. And in both senses the Church claims freedom as a strict right. In the sense of the Declaration the object or content of the right is negative — an immunity from coercive constraint or restraint by any human power in society or state, whether in the exercise of spiritual authority or in the communal living of the Christian life.

It should be noted here that the freedom of the Church is understood in this same sense in *Christus dominus,* the Decree on the Pastoral Office of Bishops: "In the performance of their apostolic office, which looks to the salvation of souls, bishops per se possess full and perfect freedom and independence of any civil power. Wherefore it is not permissible to impede, directly or indirectly, the exercise of their ecclesiastical office or to prohibit their free communication with the Apostolic See, with other ecclesiastical authorities, and with their subjects" (n. 19). Here the freedom of the Church as a spiritual authority is presented as an immunity. This concept, here as in *Dignitatis humanae,* is technically correct.

A more detailed description of the meaning of the freedom of the Church is given in the section of the Declaration which deals with religious freedom as a corporate right. This section was written with a view to satisfying the requirements both of the freedom of the Catholic Church (as set forth, for instance,

in Leo XIII) and also of the freedom of the churches and ecclesial communities (as set forth in the declarations of the
World Council of Churches, notably at Amsterdam in 1948 and
at New Delhi in 1961). Two general areas of freedom are distinguished. The first includes the internal affairs of the community — its organization, manner of rule, worship, religious
nurture, the selection, training, appointment, and transferral of
ministers, communications *ad extra*, the erection of churches,
the possession of property. The second includes the external action of the community — its public witness to its own faith as
such, and its further witness to the values of its faith in their
relation to the affairs of the temporal order. The Declaration
makes no concessions to an "angelist" conception of religion or
to the notion of churches as being shut up "in the sacristy."

Furthermore, the Declaration makes sufficiently clear —
without being altogether as precise as might be desired — that
the foundation of the Catholic Church's right to freedom is
twofold. The theological foundation is the mandate of Christ
to preach His gospel and to observe His commandments (n. 13).
This unique theological title, however, cannot be urged in political society and against government. The mandate of Christ
to His Church is formally a truth of the transcendent order in
which the authority of the Church is exercised and her life as
a community is lived. Therefore it is not subject, or even acces-
sible, to judgment by secular powers as regards its truth or
falsity. The authorities and faithful of the Church are indeed
conscious that their freedom is of divine origin — a participation
respectively in the freedom of the Incarnate Word and in the
freedom of the Holy Spirit. In political society, however, and in
the face of government, only that title to freedom may be urged
which the powers of the secular order are able, and are obliged,
to recognize. This title is the basic truth about the dignity of the
human person and about the necessary freedom of his life —
especially his religious life, both personal and corporate — in
society.

This distinction between the Church's two different titles to freedom is of the highest importance. If the unique theological title is not asserted, the way is opened to indifferentism — the reduction of the Catholic Church to one of many ecclesial communities, whose respective rights to freedom rest on univocally the same foundation, namely, a divine mandate. On the other hand, if the theological title is asserted against secular powers in society and state, the way is opened to a confusion of the two orders of human life — to a negation of the transcendence of the Church and to a violation of the due autonomy of the secular order, as this autonomy was defined by the Council rather more sharply than ever before (a matter to be dealt with later).

The Church would abdicate her transcendence, were she to present her theological title to freedom in society for judgment by any organs of secular government. As has been said, the Declaration itself makes sufficiently clear that secular government today — given the developed differentiation of the secular and sacral orders — is not empowered to make judgments *de meritis* in matters of theological truth. At the same time, the due autonomy of the secular order would be violated, since this autonomy requires that the powers which rule the secular order should make judgments on the secular grounds proper to that order — the truth which is its foundation, the justice which is its goal, the love or civic friendship which is its motivating and unifying force, the freedom which is at once its goal and its method of pursuing the goal of justice. Hence the autonomy of the secular order requires that, within this order and in the face of its constituted organs of government, the Church should present her claim to freedom on these secular grounds —in the name of the human person, who is the foundation, the end, and the bearer of the whole social process.

It should be noted too that the distinction here in question is of the highest ecumenical importance. On the one hand, it establishes the churches and ecclesial communities on a basis of reciprocity, both with regard to the object or content of their right to freedom in the social and political order, and also with regard to the foundation of this right as asserted within this order. On the other hand, this reciprocity, precisely because it is an affair only of the political and social order, implies no blurring or leveling of the doctrinal differences among the churches, which are of quite another order. As the Decree on Ecumenism says, and as all convinced Christian believers agree: "Nothing is so foreign to the spirit of ecumenism as a false irenicism which harms the purity of Catholic doctrine and obscures its assured genuine meaning" (n. 11). At the same time, the rules of the dialogue must be such that "each can treat with the other on a footing of equality" (n. 9). This reciprocity in the ecumenical dialogue is a matter of love and respect, not only for the other as a person, but also for the truth as possessed by each, to be understood by both. An analogy is visible here. The civil community in its most profound meaning and manner of action is itself a form of dialogue. The dialogue does not disguise, but brings to light, differences of view. But in order that it may be a proper dialogue, it is essential that each should treat with the other on a footing of equality. In the civil dialogue, which is carried on under conditions of constitutional order, this reciprocity is a matter of strict right. And the constitutional right — in our case, to equal religious freedom — is the necessary condition and firm support of the ecumenical dialogue.

A certain uneasiness or discontent was felt by some of the conciliar Fathers and theologians over the "negative" notion of religious freedom put forward by the Declaration. They would have wished it to be said that the freedom of the Church is a "positive" freedom. But surely there is here some failure to make the necessary distinction between two orders of discourse and reality.

The mandate of Christ empowers the Church to preach the gospel to every creature — to every man as a creature of God, to whom the divine message of salvation is addressed. To this empowerment or freedom of the Church there corresponds on the part of all men and all peoples an obligation to hear the word of God and to respond to it by faith as assent and consent. In this sense the content of the freedom of the Church is positive; it is a freedom "for" the preaching of the gospel. This discourse, however, moves in the transtemporal order of the history of salvation — the order of man's vertical relation, so to speak, to God acting and speaking in history through His Church. On the other hand, the technical issue of religious freedom rises in the juridical order, which is the order of horizontal interpersonal relations among men, between a man and organized society, and especially between the people — as individuals and as associated in communities, including religious communities — and the powers of government. As asserted in the interpersonal order of human rights, the freedom of the Church, whether as a community or as an authority, is and can only be negative in its content; it is a freedom "from" any manner of coercive constraint imposed by any secular power. As further guaranteed in the constitutional order of civil rights, the freedom of the Church consequently appears as an immunity. To confuse these two distinct orders of discourse, and the modes of freedom proper to each, is to run into inextricable difficulties.

One may be mentioned. Government is a power whose mode of action, like that of law, is ultimately coercive. If the freedom of the Church in the juridical order is rightly taken to be no more than an assurance against the use of governmental power, or any other secular power, in restraint of her divine mission, no difficulty arises. On the contrary, this self-denying ordinance on the part of government is a matter of obligation. This is obvious. On the other hand, if the freedom of the Church in the juridical order is taken to be some manner of positive claim on government, the claim can only be that government should use its power in furtherance of the Church's divine mission. *Quod absit.* No other positive content to the claim can be assigned. The Church cannot ask governments, as she asks men, for faith in the word of God. What she asks — all she can ask — of governments was immortally stated by Paul VI, in fidelity to the tradition and in authentic confirmation of the doctrine of *Dignitatis humanae,* when he spoke to statesmen in his discourse of December 8, 1965: "And what is it that the Church asks of you, after almost two thousand years of all manner of vicissitudes in her relations with you, the powers of earth — what is it that she asks of you today? In one of the major texts of the Council she has told you what it is. She asks of you nothing but freedom — freedom to believe and to preach her faith, freedom to love God and to serve Him, freedom to live and to bring to men her message of life."[7]

It is clear therefore that the Council renewed traditional doctrine on the relations of Church and state by restoring, in continuity with Leo XIII, the principle of the freedom of the Church to its fundamental place in the structure of the doctrine. By the same token, it is clear that the issue may no longer be argued in terms of "union" and "separation" of Church and state, or in terms of "thesis" and "hypothesis." The words 'union" and "separation" can mean, and in the course of history have meant, many things. In the modern canonist school, however, union of Church and state has at least meant the legal establishment of Catholicism as the religion of the state, to which constitutional status certain privileges normally accrue, and from which, in the case of other cults, certain civil disabilities logically follow.[8] Union in this sense is the thesis, the ideal prescribed by Catholic doctrine. In turn, separation, which means at least a constitutional situation of nonestablishment and of equal religious freedom for all, is hypothesis, a concession to circumstances, to be no more than tolerated.[9]

In the legislative history of the Declaration the issue of establishment was first mentioned in the *Relatio de animadversionibus Patrum* which was included in the fascicle with the third con-

---

[7] AAS 58 (1966) 10–11.

[8] Pius XI, Letter to Card. Gasparri, May 30, 1929, on the Lateran Pacts, in J. B. Lo Grasso, S.J. *Ecclesia et status: De mutuis officiis et iuribus fontes selecti* (Rome: Gregorian University, 1939) pp 326–27: ". . . la Relione cattolica è, e sol'essa, secondo lo Statuto ed i Trattati, la Religione dello Stato con le logiche e giuridiche consequenze di una tale situazione di diritto costitutivo . . . ," that is, other cults are only "tollerati, permessi, ammessi."

[9] This is the position stated in somewhat softened form in Chapter 9 of the original schema of the *Constitution on the Church*, which emanated from the Theological Commission in November, 1962.

ciliar schema *(textus emendatus)* presented in November, 1964. There it was said:

> The institution of religious freedom prohibits such legal intolerance as would reduce certain citizens or certain religious communities to a condition of inferiority in what concerns their civil rights in matters religious. But it does not forbid that the Catholic religion should be recognized by human law as the common religion of the citizens in a particular country — in other words, that the Catholic religion should be established by public law as the religion of the state. In such a case, however, care must be taken that from the institution of a state-religion no juridical or social consequences should be derived that would infringe the equality before public law of all citizens in religious matters. In a word, together with the institution of a state-religion the institution of religious freedom is to be maintained.

The purpose of this note was to respond to the objection of some Fathers that a declaration of general religious freedom would be at odds with the institution of establishment as approved by the Church, in practice and — according to some — by doctrine.

In response to the wishes of some Fathers, a sentence on establishment was inserted in the text of the fourth conciliar schema *(textus reemendatus)* presented in September, 1965. It read: "The institution of religious freedom does not stand in the way of special recognition being given to one religious community in the constitutional order of a society, under consideration of historical circumstances among peoples, in such wise, however, that at the same time the right of all citizens and religious communities to religious freedom be acknowledged and maintained."

This statement proved controversial. The *Relatio* of the Secretariat on the changes made in the fifth conciliar schema *(textus recognitus)* presented in October, 1965, distinguished four positions: (1) that no mention of establishment be made; (2) that the text should clearly affirm that special constitutional recognition must be given to the true religion whenever this is possible; (3) that, if the Declaration deals with establishment, it should do so in a conditional sentence; (4) that the Declaration should deal with establishment but in a conditional sentence. The Secretariat voted to accept the fourth proposal as the *via media*. Hence the fifth schema was made to read thus: "If, under consideration of historical circumstances among peoples, special civil recognition is given to one religious community in the constitutional order of a society, it is necessary at the same time that the right of all citizens and religious communities to religious freedom should be acknowledged and maintained" (n. 6).

After the vote of October 26, 1965, some sixteen *modi* dealing with this sentence were submitted. One of them, signed by three Fathers, asked that the whole sentence be stricken out. Another, signed by twenty-eight Fathers, asked that the sentence be changed from its conditional form back to its former declarative form. The rest proposed merely verbal alterations. The two significant changes were rejected by the Secretariat on grounds of the overwhelming vote of approval given to the section in question (2,034 to 186). Hence the final text retains the conditional form.

It is therefore clearly the mind of the Council that the establishment of Catholicism as the religion of the state is no more than a matter of historical circumstances, and not a matter — or even a consequence — of doctrine. It is not thesis but hypothesis. In fact, the conditional form of the conciliar statement, taken in its full force and in the light of the interventions of the Fathers who recommended it, reveals the unwillingness of the Council to approve the institution of establishment even as a matter of purely historic right. On the other hand, it is even more clearly the mind of the Council that the institution of religious freedom is not hypothesis but thesis — a matter of doctrine, not of historical circumstances. To put the whole thing more simply, it is time now to drop the categories of thesis and hypothesis completely out of the Catholic vocabulary. The future systematization of Catholic doctrine on Church and state will not have the disjunctive structure characteristic of the once-received opinion. Its structure will be unitary.

Moreover, it will have to be more than a doctrine on "Church and state." The traditional rubric accurately defined the issue only in the days when the Church was, or was considered to be, coterminous with society, and when a single structure of spiritual authority confronted a single structure of temporal authority. The Council, by its recognition of religious pluralism in the world (in the conciliar sense of "world"), acknowledged that this historical situation no longer exists, if it ever really did exist. The same acknowledgement is implicit also in the very notion of the "pilgrim Church," which was a dominant conciliar theme. The traditional rubric may still be useful to designate the contemporary issue, if its terms are invested with a symbolic meaning and used to designate the poles of that permanent tension in human society which reflects the tension inherent in the dual nature of man, who is a creature both of time and of eternity. However, after *Dignitatis humanae* and *Gaudium et spes*, the literal terms of the issue are rather "religion and government," religion in a historical-pluralist sense, and government in the constitutional sense accepted by these two conciliar documents, following *Pacem in terris*. This narrow issue, moreover, exists at the interior of, and in subordination to, the larger problematic of "religion and human society," already described.

The relationship of religion and government was regarded by *Dignitatis humanae* both as a theological-religious issue and also as a constitutional and legal issue. And the relationship was primarily defined in terms of freedom — the freedom of the human person and the freedom of religious communities, including the Church. The Declaration, in effect, affirmed the independence of "Church" and "state." But the notion of independence does not exhaust the issue of the relationship between these two social magnitudes, which are also structures of authority (in diverse ways, of course). Does their independence imply their separation — and what is the meaning of "separation"? Does it imply the neutrality of government toward religion, and what kind of "neutrality" — a neutrality of indifference or of general benevolence? Does it imply reciprocal cooperation and mutual support — and to what extent and in what forms? These are complex questions, and the Declaration did not undertake to deal with them adequately.

There was, however, among some of the Fathers a fear that the Declaration might be interpreted in the separationist sense of Continental laicism, which implied either hostility or at best indifference toward religion on the part of government. There was little, if any, basis for this fear, unless the concept of religious freedom in the Declaration were to be egregiously misunderstood. At any rate, in order to preclude the possibility of misinterpretation, a half sentence was added in the sixth and final conciliar schema: "Government, whose proper function is to care for the common temporal good, ought indeed to recognize the religious life of its citizens and to favor it . . ." (n. 3). Later, moreover, when it is a question of the duties of government, two are noted. The primary duty is toward the religious freedom of all citizens. The second duty is "to supply conditions favorable to the cultivation of religious life, in such wise that citizens may in fact be enabled to exercise their religious rights and to discharge their religious duties, and that society itself may enjoy the values of justice and peace which ensue upon the fidelity of men toward God and His holy will" (n. 6).

It must be admitted that this second duty is not phrased with entirely luminous clarity. Nevertheless, the intention of the statement is clear enough. It is primarily negative, that is, it is meant to exclude either a hostile or an indifferent attitude toward religion on the part of government. However, the positive meaning of the statement was deliberately left vague. What do governmental "recognition" and "favor" of religion in society concretely mean? In particular, what manner of constitutional or statutory transcription of such recognition and favor should be made? Again, what is concretely meant by "conditions favorable to religious life"? The text leaves these concrete questions open, because the answer to them would largely depend on variants.

The positive intention, however, is not in doubt. It was to affirm the traditional doctrine that religion is a social good, a fundamental element of the common temporal good of society. This was the doctrine upon which Leo XIII endlessly insisted. Religion is not simply an affair of the internal forum of conscience or even of the sacristy. It is formally a matter of public interest. Consequently, it claims the recognition and the favorable attention of government. Leo XIII was speaking, of course, about the Catholic religion, in the face of the laicizing governments of Continental Europe. The Declaration develops his doctrine by clearly stating that governmental recognition and favor of religion in society are to be accorded under safeguard of the principles of religious freedom and of the equality of all citizens before the law — an equality which "itself is integral to the common good of society" (n. 6). Therefore not only are hostility and indifference excluded; so too is "discrimination" on religious grounds (n. 6). This latter exclusion was necessary in order that the Declaration might be faithful to the Pian and Johannine (not Leonine) notion of the common good — that its primary component is juridical.

For the rest, it would seem to be in the sense of the Declaration to say that governmental favor of religion formally means favor of the freedom of religion. Similarly, conditions favorable to religious life should be understood to mean conditions favorable to the free profession and practice of religion. Government does not stand in the service of religious truth, as an instrument for its defense or propagation. Government, however, must somehow stand in the service of religion as an indispensable element of the common temporal good. This duty of service is discharged by service rendered to the freedom of religion in society. It is religion itself, not government, which has the function of making society religious. The conditions favorable to the fulfillment of this function are conditions of freedom. In the way of sheer principle, it seems not possible to say more than this. And this much the Declaration says.

GAUDIUM ET SPES

The *Constitution on the Church in the World Today* reveals a sharper sense of the distinction between society and state than can be found in Leo XIII, or perhaps even in Pius XII, though the latter, in virtue of his concern for the juridical order of society, began to sort out the confusions visible in the former. The *Constitution* deals with our question roughly in terms of this distinction. In Part 1, Chapter 4, there is question of the relation of the Church to human society and of her function in human society. In Part 2, Chapter 4, the narrower question comes up, "Church and state." In neither case is the treatment systematic; but some important principles are stated.

In dealing with the Church-and-society problematic, two major concerns seem to pervade the *Constitution.* One is to reaffirm the Leonine distinction between the two societies and likewise to reaffirm the transcendence of the Church to the temporal order. The mission of the Church, it is said, "is not of the political, economic, or social order; the purpose which [Christ] set for it is of the religious order" (n. 42). In consequence, the Church "is not bound to any particular form of human culture, or to any political, economic, or social system" *(loc. cit.).* In further consequence, her ardent wish is "that, standing in the service of the good of all, she may be able to develop freely under any form of government which recognizes the fundamental rights of the person and of the family, and also recognizes the exigencies of the common good" *(loc. cit.).*

The statement adds a new breadth and an important qualification to Leo XIII's oft-repeated thesis of the indifference of the Church to political forms. Leo XIII, in the face of the French Catholic Right, was endeavoring to disentangle the Church from the institution of monarchy, without at the same time committing the Church to democratic institutions, about which he knew nothing, except insofar as these institutions. appeared, in vitiated and unacceptable form, in the laicist republics of Continental Europe. The Council, in contrast, accepting and prolonging the views of Pius XII and of John XXIII, makes a political commitment, however discreet, to constitutional government — or, if you will, to the juridical state — whose basic inspiration is a consciousness of the dignity of the person and a recognition of human rights. Only under this manner of government is the freedom of the Church, together with the freedom of man himself, assured. Hence the Council utters one of its few rebukes: "Disapproval is voiced of (*reprobantur*) those forms of government, to be found in some countries, which fetter civil and religious freedom . . ." (n. 73). And again: "It is inhuman that political authority should assume totalitarian or dictatorial forms which do injury to the rights of the person or of associations" (n. 75).

To the transcendence of the Church are linked both the universality of her mission and her freedom in its accomplishment. However, transcendence to the world does not mean isolation from the world. The second major concern of the Constitution is to make this clear. The Council espouses the thesis of St. Augustine, developed in his treatise *De civitate Dei*, which Leo XIII had summed up in the opening paragraph of *Immortale Dei* and thereafter had endlessly repeated: "That immortal work of a merciful God, which is the Church, does indeed, per se and of its very nature, look to the salvation of souls and to their achievement of happiness in heaven. Nevertheless, in the world of mortal man it is the source of so many and such great benefits that it could not have brought forth more or greater benefits if it had been instituted, primarily and chiefly, to further the prosperity of life here on earth."[10] This is the traditional paradox.

The *Constitution* points to the resolution of it in the notion of the Church as "the leaven and, as it were, the soul of human society, which is to be renewed in Christ and transformed into the family of God." The relationship between the two Cities is described by the word "compenetration." And it is forthrightly stated that this dynamic relationship "can be perceived

---

[10] Encyclical *Immortale Dei*, Nov. 1, 1885 (Bonne Presse 2, 16).

only by faith; it is, in fact, the mystery of human history"
(n. 40).

At least the structure of the mystery can be described in these
terms: "In pursuit of her salvific purpose, the Church communi-
cates the divine life to men — but not only that; a reflection of her
light somehow streams forth over the whole world, and its effect
is chiefly shown in that it heals and elevates the dignity of the
human person, strengthens the bonds of human society, and in-
vests the daily activity of man with a deeper meaning and import"
(n. 40). The terms are Augustinian and Leonine, but with a difference. The theme of human dignity has now become central in a
new way: "By no human law can the personal dignity and freedom of man be so adequately safeguarded as by the gospel of
Christ committed to the Church" (n. 41). Or again: "In virtue of
the gospel committed to her, the Church proclaims the rights of
man; she also acknowledges and holds in high regard the
dynamism of today, whereby these rights are everywhere pro-
moted" (*loc. cit.*).

There is more than a hint of triumphalism in the first part of
this last sentence, though it is qualified by the second part. It
would be fair to say that the Church — that is, the hierarchy and
the Holy See — did nothing to advance the struggle for the political rights of man in the eighteenth and nineteenth centuries —
those rights, notably the right of free speech, which safeguard the
person against the encroachments of the state and also secure for
citizens a share in the processes of government. Only rather
late — with *Rerum novarum* in 1891 — did the papacy enter the
battle for the socioeconomic rights of man. And it was not until
Vatican II, of course, that the Church proclaimed the right to
religious freedom. The victories won in the West for the cause
of constitutional government and the rights of man owed little to
the Church, however much the "leaven of the gospel," as *Dignitatis humanae* insinuates (n. 12), may have contributed to the rise
of the secular dynamism which, in fact, brought the "free world"
into existence.

In any event, the statements in *Gaudium et spes,* like those in

Dignitatis humanae, represent *aggiornamento.* And they are pro-grammatic for the future. From now on, the Church defines her mission in the temporal order in terms of the realization of human dignity, the promotion of the rights of man, the growth of the human family towards unity, and the sanctification of the secular activities of this world.

This mission in the temporal order, however, still remains a mission of the religious order — a spiritual mission. It is limited in its scope as it is limited in the means of its accomplishment. These are entirely of the spiritual order: "The power which the Church is able to impart to human society today consists in faith and love made operative in life. It does not consist in any sort of external control exercised by merely human means" (n. 42). Here, of course, would be the place to outline the doctrine of the Decree on the Apostolate of the Laity, *Apostolicam actuositatem,* on the laity as the proper agent for the accomplishment of the mission of the Church in the temporal order. However, a mere reference to this doctrine must here suffice.

The discourse of *Gaudium et spes* on the life of the political community (Part 2, Chapter 4) is uninspired and inadequate. For instance, there is no mention of the cardinal political principle of the consent of the governed, which is as old as Aristotle and Cicero, and which was central to the political thought of the High Middle Ages, even though the institutions to make it operative were lacking at that time. So too the section on the political community and the Church (n. 76) does no more than state a few general principles. At that, these are stated in such a way as to exhibit nuances of development.

Mention is made of the "pluralist society" (an almost last-minute addition to the text). It is suggested that this type of so-ciety gives rise to today's problem of the relations of Church and state. There is, however, no firm affirmation that the pluralist society presents not only the normal but also the normative con-text for any theory of these relations. The wider state of the question, "religion and government," which was implicitly ad-opted by *Dignitatis humanae,* is here contracted to the dimensions exhibited in the introductory rubric, "the political community and the Church." The narrowness of this view was probably necessary, but it was also regrettable.

The first assertion, here as earlier, bears on the transcendence of the Church to the political community and its various forms. The earlier idea of "compenetration" also appears, if only implicitly, in the statement that the Church "is at the same time the sign and safeguard of the transcendence of the human person" (n. 76). It is characteristic of *Gaudium et spes* that it occasionally strikes off a brilliant phrase, pregnant with implications, in the midst of a passage of otherwise prolix and uninspired prose. This is such a phrase. Its implications are extensive. It suggests the central significance of the Church for the political order. It suggests the *locus standi* of the Church in the face of the state — the order of public law and administration. It suggests the essential basis of the Church's claim to freedom in the face of all public powers. It implies that the Church may neither be enclosed within the political order nor be denied her own mode of spiritual entrance into the political order. It indirectly asserts the rightful secularity of the secular order, at the same time it asserts the necessary openness of the secular order to the transcendent values whose pursuit is proper to the human person. If one were looking for a single phrase in which to resolve the whole problematic of *Gaudium et spes* — the dynamic relation of the Church to the world — this might well be the phrase, especially if it were understood that for the Church to signify and safeguard the transcendence of the human person is for her likewise to signify and further the unity of the human family.

The text does not fully draw out all these implications. It goes on briefly to reaffirm the Leonine principle: "The political community and the Church are independent of each other, and are autonomous, each in its own field" (n. 76). It further proceeds to reaffirm the principle, likewise Leonine, of their necessary harmony — except that it uses the word "cooperation" instead of the favorite Leonine word "concord." There is, however,

an interesting nuance in the statement of the necessity for this
concord or cooperation. For Leo, the reason lay in the fact that
the two structures of authority, for all their independence as
structures, held command and rule over the same body of men
— the same one man who is "at once citizen and Christian." As
Libertas puts it: "Utriusque est in eosdem imperium."[11] For
Leo XIII, authority is rule. For the Council, however, authority
is service: "Both [authorities], though on a different title, stand
in the service of the personal and social vocation of the same
men" (n. 76). This restatement of the Leonine doctrine reflects
the more personalist conception, to call it such, both of the
People of God and of the People Temporal.

The principle of cooperation of Church and state in the service
of the human person is thus stated as a principle. However,
the concrete forms of cooperation are to be instituted "under regard for circumstances of place and time" (n. 76). Implicit, here
again, is a rejection of the disjunctive theory and its assertion
of an abstract "thesis." Explicit is a recognition that the contingent relativities of history, and not any logical deductions from
abstract principle, must determine the institutional forms of
Church-state cooperation. Moreover, the rest of the paragraph
makes it clear that the cooperation, both as a matter of principle and in the various forms of its realization, is not required
by some sort of *raison d'église* but by the dual nature of the
human person: "Man is not confined to the temporal order
alone; rather, living his life in human history, he has a care for
his eternal vocation in its wholeness" (n. 76).

Therefore, it is implied, the care of the Church extends in
diverse ways to both aspects of man's destiny, since man is a
unity and his destiny is somehow unitary. However, the limitations of the mission of the Church in the temporal order are
again stated and all manner of clericalism is again rejected by
this assertion: "Those who give themselves to the ministry of
the word of God must make use of ways and means which are

[11] Encyclical *Libertas praestantissimum*, June 20, 1888 (Bonne Presse
2, 192).

proper to the gospel and these differ in many respects from the means at the disposal of the earthly city" (n. 76).

Finally, the *Constitution* comes to the principle of the freedom of the Church:

> It is always and everywhere necessary that [the Church] should preach the faith with true freedom, teach her doctrine about society, exercise her function among men without hindrance, and pass moral judgment even on affairs that belong to the political order, when such judgment is required by concern for the fundamental rights of the person or for the salvation of souls, under use of all those means, and only those means, which are in harmony with the gospel and with the good of all, having regard for diversities of time and place (n. 76).

This statement of what the freedom of the Church means is not as extensive and complete as the statement made in *Dignitatis humanae*. However, in accord with its own context, it lays emphasis on the point less emphatically made in *Dignitatis humanae*, namely, the Church's freedom of spiritual entrance into the order of politics. The mode of entrance is purely spiritual, since it takes the form simply of moral judgment on political affairs, and since the grounds of judgment are metapolitical, having to do with the rights of man and the salvation of souls. Moreover, nothing is here said about the execution of these moral judgments in terms of law, public policy, social action, etc. On this crucial point the *Constitution* is content to have recalled a necessary distinction, "between those affairs which Christians, whether alone or in association, undertake as citizens, under the guidance of their Christian conscience, and those affairs which Christians undertake in the name of the Church and in union with their pastors" (n. 76). This distinction, one may think, is rather distinctively European in its origin and import. It began to come into currency in the twenties, under Pius XI, when there began to be talk of Catholic Action (with the initial letters in upper case), which is a form of organized apostolate not common outside the Latin countries.

In the context of discourse both about the evangelical character of the Church's resources and about the freedom of the Church, the *Constitution* makes a further important point, both of principle and of practice: "The Church does not put her trust in privileges granted by civil authority. More than that, she will renounce the exercise of certain legitimately acquired rights, when it shall have become clear that their exercise may call into question the disinterested character of her witness, or when new circumstances of life require different arrangements" (n. 76). The implicit disavowal of the ancient recourse to the secular arm is clear enough. The notion that certain rights of the Church can be merely historic — therefore contingently legitimate but not exigencies of doctrine — is likewise clear enough. But the privileges in question are not specified. Perhaps it may be permissible to see a reference to the modern right to legal establishment asserted within the nation-state, and to other consequent legal privileges. Thus the doctrine of *Dignitatis humanae* would be fittingly completed.

In any event, the sharpened awareness of the purely spiritual character of the Church's mission, even in the temporal order, which is visible all through the *Constitution*, leads necessarily to a new disposition on the part of the Church to impose self-denying ordinances on the whole range of her action within the temporal order. This new disposition is part of that spirit of evangelical poverty about which the conciliar Fathers frequently discoursed.

It is in place here to cite the invitation issued by *Christus Dominus* to civil authorities that they should likewise pass some self-denying ordinances:

> Consequently, in order rightly to protect the freedom of the Church and more fittingly and effectively to promote the good of the faithful, the Council desires that in the future no rights or privileges regarding the choice, nomination, presentation, or designation for the episcopal office should be granted to civil authorities. Moreover, civil authorities themselves, whose obedient disposition toward the Church the Council gratefully acknowledges, are courteously asked to renounce, of their own

accord and after consultation with the Holy See, rights of this kind which they presently enjoy by compact or custom (n. 20).

The premise of this request was the stated doctrine that "the right of nominating and installing bishops is the proper, peculiar, and per se exclusive right of competent ecclesiastical authority" (loc. cit.).

The tendency of the request itself is to realize more perfectly the implications of the principle stated by Leo XIII: "It cannot be doubted, under safeguard of the faith, that the governance of souls was committed to the Church alone, in such wise that powers of the political order have no share whatever in it."[12] The historic privilege of governments to nominate bishops was, however remotely and subtly, a share in the governance of souls. It was always per se an abuse, a confusion of the secular and sacral orders, and, as the Council clearly implied, an infringement of the freedom of the Church, an invasion of her immunity from political interference in all that concerns her own internal government and her care of souls.

The simple conclusion here is that the two conciliar documents, *Dignitatis humanae* and *Gaudium et spes*, have made a joint contribution toward the renewal of traditional doctrine with regard to the ancient issue of Church and state. Previous confusions of the historical with the doctrinal have been sorted out. The systematization based on the distinction between thesis and hypothesis has been dismantled. The relevant principles have been stated with a new purity, which was made possible by the new perspectives in which the whole issue was viewed. New theological insights into the concrete reality of the pilgrim Church, and other new insights made available by secular experience (notably the experience of the relation between religious freedom as a human right and the freedom of the Church), have resulted in genuine and fruitful development of doctrine. This doctrinal work was inspired by the maxim of Leo XIII, "Vetera novis augere et perficere." A work of systematization remains to be done under the same inspiration.

---

[12] Encyclical *Sapientiae christianae*, Jan. 10, 1890 (Bonne Presse 2, 283).

CHAPTER V

THE COUNCIL, THE FAMILY,
AND THE COMMUNITY OF MAN

John L. Thomas, S.J.

It is not surprising to find references to the family in most documents of Vatican II. As the basic unit of society, the family fulfills a number of significant functions having far-reaching personal and social implications for the Christian community and the success of the Church's mission. What does seem somewhat surprising in the light of contemporary conditions is that the several commissions charged with drafting tentative texts for consideration by a Council that was called to be pastoral apparently did not recognize the need to prepare a separate text on marriage and the family. The Council Fathers partially remedied this oversight in Part II of their *Pastoral Constitution on the Church in the Modern World* by including marriage and the family among the "subjects arousing universal concern today" and devoting Chapter I to their considerations relating to "Fostering the Nobility of Marriage and the Family."

This chapter of the *Constitution* is clearly not intended to provide a complete treatise on the Church's teaching concerning marriage and the family; rather, its aims as stated are much more modest, "by presenting certain key points of Church doctrine in a clearer light, this Council wishes to offer guidance and support to those Christians and other men who are trying to keep sacred and to foster the natural dignity of the married state and its superlative value" (Art. 47). This somewhat limited approach was not dictated solely by the pastoral aims of the Council. As footnote 14 reminds us, "certain questions which need further and more careful investigation have been handed over, at the command of the Supreme Pontiff, to a commission for the study of population, family, and births, in order that, after it fulfills its function, the Supreme Pontiff may pass judgment. With the doctrine of the magisterium in this state, this holy Synod does not intend to propose immediately concrete solutions."

Although considerable secrecy and consequent uncertainty have surrounded the workings of this special commission, it appears that the Council Fathers interpreted the scope of its functions to be rather broad. Hence, while insisting that the faithful must accept the "teaching authority of the Church in its unfolding of the divine law," they consistently refrained from making any new pronouncements regarding the morality of various types of contraceptive intervention relating to the marital act and the reproductive process. Further, through a judicious choice of terms in speaking about the purposes of marriage they clearly indicated that they regarded questions relating to the hierarchy of ends as well as the adequacy of traditional terminology and formulations to be among the "certain questions" handed over to Pope Paul's special commission for study.

In spite of these restrictions, the documents of Vatican II indicate considerable development in the Church's official thinking and teaching on marriage and the family. Stated briefly, there is evidence of a more adequate understanding of the human dimensions of marriage, particularly in regard to conjugal love, sexual relations, and responsible parenthood. Since some of the faithful are apparently upset by any indication of change or development in the Church's official teaching, while others feel that change is long overdue, it may not be out of place to point out at once why the Church has always experienced a good deal of difficulty in trying to clarify its official stand regarding marriage and the family.

In the first place, the family is a wholly secular reality, and being fully human, it is open to change, development, and gradual evolution. The Church did not found the family. She regards it as a natural society, an institution of nature, in the sense that some form of community between parents and children is required by human nature and consequently arises spontaneously wherever men exist. The mutually complementary sexual nature of men and women as well as the relatively helpless condition of the human infant at birth involve fundamental needs that can adequately be satisfied only in the family. As a matter of fact, although the major functions fulfilled by the family are separable from one another and could conceivably be carried out by separate institutions, they are not separated in any known major family system.

This close relationship between the family and the requirements of nature accounts for the functional similarities common to all stable family systems. For example, all systems include some form of mating relationship through which men and women are brought together for purposes of procreating; some form of marriage ceremony or social arrangement by means of which this mating relationship becomes publicly recognized and duly acknowledged by the community; some definite habitat, household or home in which this marital unit is localized; some organized provision for the satisfaction of the material and psychic needs associated with childbearing and the nurturing of offspring; and finally, some type of kinship system designating how persons sharing various relationships based on marriage or common descent are related to members of a given family unit and to each other.

Apart from these common general elements, however, family systems may differ considerably, depending on available cultural and physical resources, current definitions of sex and parenthood, and underlying conceptions of human nature. Such differences reflect the various ways that men have found more or less satisfactory in fulfilling their sexual and parental needs. The range of possibilities in this regard is extensive but not without definite limitations based on the requirements of nature. The family is a natural society in the sense that although a given family system appears as a cultural product, it is the dual sexual quality of human nature together with the helplessness of the human infant which constitute the unchanging, natural elements that set limits to the range of cultural determinations in every instance.

When the Church entered the Hellenic world, she possessed no clearly defined, specifically Christian conception of the family. The early Christians lived in the family before they began to theorize about its nature or essential elements. Whether as Jews or gentiles, they were drawn from long-established family systems, within which they had been raised, were currently involved and for the most part continued to live. As a spiritual movement, Christianity did not attempt to destroy or replace these family systems; yet the Gospel Message relating to chastity, the equality of the sexes before God, the value of human life and the sanctity and stability of the marriage bond exerted a gradual leavening force on the attitudes and practices of all who accepted it. As Christianity spread, the need to evaluate various alien family systems as well as to refute numerous heretical tendencies among the faithful forced Church teachers to clarify their thinking and make more explicit some of the practical implications and profound spiritual dimensions of the Gospel Message relating to marriage and the family. The conception that finally emerged was a synthesis of Hellenic, Jewish, Christian, and Teutonic elements which Catholic theologians and canon lawyers had gradually shaped into a fairly consistent system of beliefs, values, principles, and practical norms embodying the Church's basic teaching on sex, love, and marriage.

I have introduced these brief historical observations because they throw some light on the second difficulty the Church faces in dealing with marriage. According to Catholic doctrine, the family is a wholly secular human reality, and as we have indicated, is open to change and development. More important, however, this reality touches salvation intimately, not only because Christians must experience it in their lives in the world but primarily because it has been incorporated by the Savior into the economy of salvation and constitutes a formal sacrament. Thus the Church faces the perennial challenge of analyzing and understanding the evolving form and functioning of this reality, for it is precisely this integral human reality and not a neat juridical abstraction that becomes in the marriage of baptized Christians the sign or sacrament of the mystery of the living communion between Christ and his Church.

Those among the faithful who are upset by any thought of change or development in the Church's official teaching on marriage and family problems appear quite innocent of history and consequently remain unaware that they are identifying the complex integral human reality constituting marriage and the family with certain historically developed juridical and ethical abstractions. Granting that the current reaction to "legalism" in theology entails its own special difficulties, it could prove beneficial to the extent that it serves to remind theologians that they cannot deal with the human realities of marriage and sex in *apartheid*.

On the basis of these considerations we may conclude that there are two basic questions which we must keep in mind when studying the Council's contribution to the Church's official teaching on marriage and the family. First, do the documents indicate any development in the Church's understanding of the contemporary family and its problems? Second, considering the restrictions imposed on the Council by the Supreme Pontiff, do its pronouncements provide any new theological insights or emphases that might serve as basic starting points for the development of a more adequately Christian interpretation of the complex human realities involved in marriage and family life? In formulating these questions, I have proceeded on the assumption that the worth of a pastoral council's contributions will depend to a major degree on the added understanding of current facts and doctrinal principles they reflect.

Did the Council Fathers make any contributions to our understanding of the current family situation? In Chapter I, Part II, of *The Pastoral Constitution on the Church in the Modern World*, after mentioning the supreme importance of the family, they outline a number of reasons why the excellence of this institution is not everywhere reflected with equal brilliance. "For polygamy, the plague of divorce, so-called free love, and other disfigurements have an obscuring effect. In addition, married love is too often profaned by excessive self-love, the worship of pleasure, and illicit practices against human generation. Moreover, serious disturbances are caused in families by modern economic conditions, by influences at once social and psychological, and by the demands of civil society. Finally, in certain parts of the world problems resulting from population growth are generating concern" (Art. 47). Although the somewhat disparate items in this general catalogue may be regarded as broadly relevant, their present relative significance is not clear, for with the possible exception of the last statement relating to population pressure, they could have been mentioned by any council in the Church's history.

What we expect from a pastoral council is something much more specific to our age. If the family is a human reality subject to change and development, and if, considered as a social institution, it necessarily affects and is affected by all relevant elements in its social environment, we may take it for granted that each historical type of family organization will involve its own peculiar stresses and strains and each generation of couples will face their own special problems. In other words, although every ongoing family system must fulfill the two essential functions of regulating sexual behavior for purposes of reproduction and providing for the integral development or socialization of offspring, the special problems associated with the attainment of these basic family objectives will stem not only or primarily from normal human weakness but from the specific culturally and socially conditioned means through which these objectives are currently to be achieved.

To be sure, in its official teaching the Church has always tended to emphasize broad family objectives, maintaining that only the stable family, that is, the family founded on a permanent, exclusive, indissoluble union, adequately provides for the fitting development and expression of mature creative love; and only the community of life and love thus established can fully supply the nurturing domestic environment within which children can be reared to assume full adult status in society and the Mystical Body. Nevertheless, while affirming, or better, perhaps, because she affirms, the crucial significance of the family in the development and destiny of man — for the family socializes him as a child and determines the basic framework of relationships within which he fulfills himself as an adult — the Church must also be concerned with the maintenance of adequate implementing means. These are relative to the environment, subject to change, frequently open to alternatives, and consequently cannot be deduced *a priori* solely from the nature of man or his institutional objectives but must be constantly redefined, adjusted, and adapted in terms of the total evolving human context. Thus in order to judge the morality of these various implementing means, the Church must seriously study the evolving form and functioning of the family in its changing environment, being careful to distinguish ends from means, lest she fall into the seemingly endemic religious error of identifying a particular historical expression of the family with the Christian ideal and thus come to regard both ends and means as divinely established absolutes.

As I have mentioned, the documents of Vatican II offer several indications that some of the Council Fathers, at least, had considerable understanding of the current family situation. Stated briefly, there is encouraging evidence of increased awareness that serious population problems exist or are presently shaping up in some of the developing countries; that many fertile couples in all modern societies are finding it increasingly difficult to reconcile their normal expressions of conjugal love with the requirements of responsible parenthood; and finally, that changes in the organization of society and the structure of the family are augmenting the social status of women as well as the strategic significance of conjugal love in maintaining the stability of marriage and the family.

Let us begin with what the Council has to say about problems relating to rapid population growth. It must be admitted that up to Vatican II the official documents of the Church have revealed a peculiar reluctance to face realistically the far-reaching individual and social implications of modern population trends. Despite the necessarily hypothetical character of past estimates and the admitted inadequacy of most contemporary vital statistics, particularly in the developing countries, it is becoming increasingly clear that the population of the world has grown at an unprecedented rate during the past several centuries and possesses the potential of even faster development. Since there is little evidence for assuming widespread variation in the natural ability to procreate, it should be obvious that the traditional checks of disease, famine, and war no longer serve as effective controls on rapid population growth. Granted current nuptiality rates, age at marriage, and advances in health care, no sizable modern nation can long make reasonable provision for its population increases unless a good percentage of its fertile couples take some effective steps to regulate family size.

The profound implications of this change have been partially obscured in the industrialized nations of the West because the extensive use of various types of birth control, particularly during the past century and a half, has lead to drastic reduction of birth rates. Beginning first among the upper classes and then gradually diffusing downward, attitudes and practices relating to birth control, formerly confined largely to social deviants or members of the demimonde, have now become an integral element of Western family culture. At present the large agrarian societies of the world, including roughly two-thirds of the current human population, are apparently reproducing at near capacity levels, while the widespread application of modern health techniques developed in the industrialized West is rapidly lowering death rates, primarily through control of the infectious diseases that formerly eliminated large numbers of infants and children. Since this rapidly increasing two-thirds of the world's population lives in countries producing only one-third of the world's food and even less of its industrial wealth, the existence of serious population problems can no longer be regarded as hypothetical.

Nevertheless, the official pronouncements of the Church before Vatican II reveal an almost studied refusal to come to grips with reality in discussing world population trends. For example, although the encyclical *Mater et Magistra* devotes a section to population increase and economic development, it indicates little awareness of the real dimensions of the problem. Current imbalances between population increases and production in the developing countries are regarded as temporary. Evidence for grave global difficulties is held to be inconclusive. International cooperation and fuller use of natural resources is urged. And mankind's uncontrolled reproductive capacity is so far from being regarded as a possible source of difficulty that not only are all morally objectionable forms of birth control understandably condemned but morally licit means are not even mentioned.

By contrast, the approach of the Council Fathers appears much more enlightened. When discussing international cooperation in the matter of population, they point out that many developing countries are burdened in a special way with difficulties stemming from a rapid population growth and that the minds of men are powerfully disturbed about this problem (Art. 87). Thus in addition to indicating the need for international aid and cooperation, education, and social reform, they state that government officials, "within the limits of their own competence," must be actively concerned with the various social aspects of their nation's population problems and that "especially in universities Catholic experts in all these aspects should skillfully pursue their studies and projects and give them an ever wider scope." Moreover, after warning against immoral solutions and vindicating the rights of parents in regard to begetting children, determining family size, and receiving the moral training requisite to making such decisions with a rightly formed conscience, they declare that "human beings should also be judiciously informed of scientific advances in the exploration of methods by which spouses can be helped in arranging the number of their children," adding that, "the reliability of these methods should be adequately proven and their harmony with the moral order should be clear." In other words, the whole tenor of their approach reflects an informed awareness of the problem as well as a product concern with the need to search for workable solutions.

But problems relating to population control are not confined to the developing countries. Under contemporary conditions, the spacing of pregnancies and the regulation of family size constitute more or less serious difficulties for most fertile couples in the Western world. To what extent do the Council documents reflect an understanding of the basic issues involved in this problem? Before answering this question, I feel it is relevant to recall that, judged from the viewpoint of Catholic moral standards, the fundamental issues relating to population control are essentially similar for all modern nations. Moreover, with a few minor or partial exceptions the economically developed nations of the West have not solved their population problems by following methods morally acceptable to Catholics; and if we consider the morally approved methods available at the beginning of the industrial revolution when European populations began to increase, it would be difficult to conjecture what practical forms such solutions would have assumed. It is a matter of historical record that the gap between the Church's official teaching on marital relations and the actual practice of the faithful began widening to an alarming extent well over a century ago when the effective desire for family limitation first became widespread in the industrializing nations of the West.

Awareness of this increasing gap between official teaching and actual practice should have led contemporary theologians to a serious reappraisal of the moral assumptions and premises of values upon which their doctrine was historically founded; yet they displayed little understanding of the new cultural outlooks, social conditions, and pressures which since the sixteenth century had been gradually transforming traditional attitudes toward marriage, parenthood, and children. As frequently happens when long-accepted moral standards and practices began to be widely neglected or fall under direct attack, religious leaders reacted by focusing primary effort and attention on the defense of the specific moral norms being called into question rather than on a careful re-examination of the possible inadequacy of the total doctrinal framework within which these norms were initially formulated.

Even Pius XI's classic encyclical *Casti Connubii*, with its fine sensitivity to the excellence of marriage, offered little indication of serious reappraisal in this regard; nonetheless, its statement that marital relations could be used for purposes other than procreation, together with the recent discovery of fairly reliable scientific methods of ascertaining the time of ovulation, generated widespread controversy among theologians and culminated in Pius XII's 1951 address to the Italian midwives clarifying the morality of periodic continence. Unfortunately, the majority of Church leaders remained so little aware of the true nature of the problem that even when Pope Pius XII gave rather broad approval to periodic continence, failure to encourage and support competent research, instruction, and guidance relative to the practice seriously limited its usefulness for most couples. Until the last few years, indeed, the rather general refusal to include discussions of family regulation and periodic continence in premarital and marital instructions left the average couple confused about the extent of their parental obligations, uncertain of the conditions under which the practice of periodic continence was morally licit, and woefully ignorant of the practical knowledge requisite for its effective use. In regard to this last point, I might add that the majority had, and still have, few reliable sources of information and guidance to which to turn, for the average American physician, at least, is quite unprepared to render competent service in this regard, though it appears that some attempt to do so.

Against this historical backdrop, the Council Fathers' clear recognition that a serious problem exists must be regarded as a considerable advance. Thus they state, "This Council realizes that certain modern conditions often keep couples from arranging their married lives harmoniously, and that they find themselves in circumstances where at least temporarily the size of their families should not be increased" (Art. 51). The criteria for making this decision to regulate family size had already been indicated as follows: "They will thoughtfully take into account both their welfare and that of their children, those already born and those which may be foreseen. For this accounting they will reckon with both the material and the spiritual conditions of the times as well as of their state in life. Finally, they will consult the interests of the family group, of temporal society, and of the Church herself" (Art. 50).

But what is more important, perhaps, in addition to recognizing the need for regulation and spelling out the criteria for reaching a responsible decision in this regard, the Council calls attention to some of the practical implications of such a decision for the couple, since regulation involves either absolute or periodic continence. "As a result, the faithful exercise of love and the full intimacy of their lives are hard to maintain. But where the intimacy of married life is broken off, it is not rare for its faithfulness to be imperiled and its quality of fruitfulness ruined. For then the upbringing of the children and the courage to accept new ones are both endangered" (Art. 51). As the Council Fathers see it, this is the heart of the matter: some regulation seems necessary, yet the only permissible methods pose a serious threat to the essential "goods" of marriage — fidelity, stability, and parenthood. They do not attempt to solve the dilemma, for the Pope has accepted this responsibility, yet they make it clear that they are aware of the situation and fully understand its implications. Moreover, in their concluding remarks on promoting the good estate of marriage and the family, they give a further indication of their serious concern in this regard, "Those, too, who are skilled in other sciences, notably the medical, biological, social, and psychological, can considerably advance the welfare of marriage and the family, along with peace of conscience, if by pooling their efforts they labor to explain more thoroughly the various conditions favoring a proper regulation of births" (Art. 52).

The third aspect of the current family situation concerning which the Council Fathers showed increased understanding relates to the changing status of women and the strategic significance of conjugal love. These two items are closely related, for conjugal love as presently understood not only requires *de facto* as well as *de jure* equality of partners, but the cultural and social changes making possible the enhanced status of women also weaken the external supports of marriage and consequently confer a strategic role on conjugal love in maintaining family stability. That the cultural transition required by these changes may not always proceed smoothly the Council Fathers are quite aware, for they list the "new social relationships between men and women" as one of the major sources of discord in the modern family (Art. 8).

On the positive side, the Council notes that "Where they have not yet won it, women claim for themselves an equity with men before the law and in fact" (Art. 9). It deplores the fact that fundamental personal rights are not yet being universally honored: "Such is the case of a woman who is denied the right and freedom to choose a husband, to embrace a state of life, or to acquire an education or cultural benefits equal to those recognized for men" (Art. 29). Pointing out that "women are now employed in almost every area of life," it declares that "they should be able to assume their full proper role in accordance with their own nature. Everyone should acknowledge and favor the proper and necessary participation of women in cultural life" (Art. 60). In its *Decree on the Apostolate of the Laity* the Council further states, "Since in our times women have an ever more active share in the whole life of society, it is very important that they participate more widely also in the various fields of the Church's apostolate" (Art. 9). And finally, in regard to women's role in the family, after insisting that partners should reach their decisions relating to family size "by common counsel and effort" and "with wise and common deliberation" (Art. 50), it underlines the mother's importance in the home, particularly when the children are young, but adds, "This domestic role of hers must be safely preserved, though the legitimate social progress of women should not be underrated on that account" (Art. 52). This striking evidence of the Council's concern with the equal status of women clearly reflects a refreshing awareness of contemporary trends, and I shall only add the rather trite observation that it represents something of a tardy breakthrough in the Church's official documents.

Most commenators on Vatican II have called attention to the great importance attributed to conjugal love in the Council's treatment of marriage. This esteem is not new in the sense that conjugal love was previously ignored or disregarded. However, with the exception of a passage in Pius XI's *Casti Connubii*, it had been taken more or less for granted, that is, it had not been formally conceptualized as a value meriting special attention. The Council's approach undoubtedly reflects the highly personalist accent characterizing much recent popular writing on marriage, but it may more appropriately be regarded as a long overdue official reaction to the onesided, wholly jurdical emphasis found in most formal treatises on marriage. At the same time, it may be viewed as a specific instance of the contemporary movement to focus moral concern on the human exigencies of Christian love rather than on legal constructs.

As the Council Fathers are well aware, conjugal love is not a univocal term. Our conceptions of conjugal love, as of all relationships between man and woman, are culturally conditioned and consequently admit of a wide variety of meanings and expressions. In one form or another and in varying shades of intensity, conjugal love is found in all known cultures. Particularly among the industrialized nations of the West, where considerable emphasis is placed on the equality of the sexes and on the nuclear family type with its limited formal kinship bonds and restricted family circle, love has come to be recognized as an essential element in mate selection and a prime requisite of marital happiness. Although the nuclear type family appears most consonant with the spatial and social mobility, individualism, and economic independence required by industrialization, it lacks the external support of an extended kinship group, while its contraction of meaningful familial relationships to the isolated conjugal unit greatly intensifies the emotional load and parental burdens which the individual couple must bear. Under these conditions conjugal love comes to play a strategic role in assuring the stability of marriage. Whether the Council Fathers were directly concerned with this aspect of the problem is not clear, but the central position they assign to conjugal love clearly indicates their awareness of contemporary conditions.

Let us turn now to the second question we asked about the Council's contribution to the Church's official teaching on marriage and the family. Do its pronouncements provide any new theological insights or emphases that might serve as basic starting points for the development of a more adequately Christian interpretation of the complex human realities involved in marriage and family life? Since we tend to see in a situation only those elements that through training and reflection we are prepared to see, the new understanding of the marriage and family problems we have been discussing would lead us to expect some development in theological insights and emphases. In this connection, however, we must recall that the Council Fathers were placed in a rather difficult position since several key questions had been reserved by the Supreme Pontiff for consideration by his special commission and were consequently excluded from their deliberations. These restrictions probably go far toward explaining a certain air of ambiguity, if not ambivalence, characterizing some of their pronouncements on the purposes of marriage and the regulation of family size.

Considering the long and troubled history of Christian attempts to discover the Creator's plan in regard to sex and marital relations, perhaps the Council's most significant contribution is its frank recognition and acceptance of the sexual dimensions of conjugal love. Thus after pointing out that conjugal love is "eminently human" and "involves the good of the whole person," it declares: "Therefore, it can enrich the expressions of body and mind with a unique dignity, ennobling these expressions as special ingredients and signs of the friendship distinctive of marriage. This love the Lord has judged worthy of special gifts, healing, perfecting, and exalting gifts of grace and of charity" (Art. 49). And lest there be any lingering doubts concerning the goodness of sexual relations in marriage, the Council adds, "This love is uniquely expressed and perfected through the marital act. The actions within marriage by which the couple are united intimately and chastely are noble and worthy ones. Expressed in a manner which is truly human, these actions signify and promote that mutual self-giving by which spouses enrich each other with a joyful and a thankful will" (Art. 49).

To my knowledge, these statements are unique among the Church's official documents on marriage and the family. Obviously, they do not solve all the delicate, intimate personal problems involved in achieving mature sexual adjustment in marriage, but by assigning marital relations a central role in the normal expressions of conjugal love and attributing special unifying properties to these expressions, they furnish a sound basis for a balanced Christian orientation to such problems and to human sexual relations in general. Although marital relations have probably always been more or less vaguely associated with conjugal love in the popular mind, there are a number of reasons why this association was not formally conceptualized by theologians and its practical implications were not stressed in the common "taught" tradition shaping the attitudes and practices of the faithful.

In the first place, Christian theologians have experienced great difficulty in developing an objective, conceptually integrated view of human sexuality. Thus, pre-Augustinian Christian teachers, possessing no conceptually refined, well-integrated system of moral theology and beset by various types of Gnostic, Manichaean, and Pelagian views, were chiefly preoccupied with the pastoral problems of refuting various doctrinal extremes. St. Augustine's classic definition of the "goods" of marriage could have furnished the basis for a more positive theological approach, yet his assumptions regarding sexual concupiscence and original sin prevented this. Briefly, he argued that since sexuality in fallen man was vitiated by the most virulent form of concupiscence — *libido carnalis* — the marital act was not inherently good but could only be justified by the external good of procreation. Proceeding on this assumption that sexual concupiscence was evil in itself or in its use, Christian thinkers for the next thousand years were primarily concerned with discovering extrinsic reasons for justifying marital relations and warning against their excessive enjoyment. Although more balanced countercurrents of opinion gradually began to develop during the sixteenth and seventeenth centuries, it must be admitted that Augustine's pessimistic conception of sexual concupiscence has run like a leitmotif through most past Christian thinking on sexuality and until very recent times has inhibited theologians from developing a balanced view of marital relations.

Moreover, throughout most of the past there has been little understanding or appreciation of feminine sexuality and little concern with the wife's enjoyment of marital relations. This is generally explained as the result both of excessive feminine prudery and a predominantly male-centered approach to sexuality, yet these explanations deal with symptoms rather than causes. Given the absence of adequate obstetrical assistance during childbirth and the distressingly high maternal and infant mortality rates characterizing most of the past, as well as the lack of any reliable and morally acceptable means of separating marital relations from procreation, it should be obvious that women would develop a different view of sex than men and would consequently tend to regard marital relations primarily as the prelude to inevitable suffering, sorrow, and danger. Under these circumstances, the wife's expression of conjugal love in regard to marital relations came to be defined as the dutiful proffering of the marriage "debt," an obligation to which moral theologians and spiritual directors devoted considerable attention.

Furthermore, once knowledge and acceptance of various contraceptive birth control techniques became widespread, religious teachers reacted by placing primary emphasis on the right performance of the act as the major criterion of acceptable marital relations. This concern with the negative aspects of the marital act, a typical example of that doctrinal imbalance that frequently occurs when cherished moral standards come under attack, while it did not deny or wholly ignore the normal relationship between conjugal love and marital relations, tended to leave the practical implications of this relationship largely unexplored. Thus, the inherent, built-in demands of justice and charity necessarily governing all sexual activities in marriage as a relationship between persons, together with their potentially unifying and stabilizing effects as a shared expression of love, received little direct attention until recently.

As a matter of fact, serious defense of the Church's official teaching on birth control is almost bound to involve some neglect of the human dimensions of marital relations, for the Church's position is based on an analysis of the marital act as a potentially life-transmitting act, the essential structure of which must always be respected since it signifies the Creator's intent. In this sense, the Council's statements relative to conjugal love and marital relations raise some serious questions concerning the adequacy of the Church's official teaching on birth control. If the effective fulfillment resulting from the ongoing sexual exchange built into the very intimacy of the marriage state has health-giving qualities highly significant for the maintenance of conjugal love, marital stability, companionship and communication, the observance of absolute or prolonged continence may seriously jeopardize the essential "goods" of marriage (*fides, proles, sacramentum*). As I have mentioned above, the Council Fathers were aware of this problem but did no more than call attention to it. Given the restrictions under which they labored, perhaps this is all that could be expected of them, but it lends an air of ambiguity to their entire treatment of marriage, since on the one hand they constantly warn against the use of illicit practices preventing generation, and on the other they set forth a description of conjugal love and marital relations that cannot easily be reconciled with the Church's present interpretation of what constitutes legitimate means of regulating family size.

Finally, I would like to call attention to a brief but highly relevant statement regarding a specific parental obligation. At the end of its discussion on conjugal love, the Council states, "Especially in the heart of their own families, young people should be aptly and seasonably instructed about the dignity, duty, and expression of married love. Trained thus in the cultivation of chastity, they will be able at a suitable age to enter a marriage of their own after an honorable courtship" (Art. 49). To be sure the Church has constantly insisted on the rights and obligations of parents in regard to the education and religious training of their children. Nevertheless, perhaps because of the nature of the subject, her recommendations relating to the teaching of chastity have tended to be somewhat vague, unrealistic, and not a little tainted with what one might describe as latent Latin Manichaeism.

At any rate, experience and research show that the majority of Catholic parents are either incapable or unwilling to instruct "aptly and seasonably" their children about the dignity, duty, and expression of married love, as the Council recommends. Even if we take the most scientifically conservative view of the current sex revolution, we must conclude that developing a positive program of instruction and training in chastity constitutes one of the major challenges Christians face today. Although the Council Fathers do not spell out the details of such a program, the positive value they attribute to marital relations as an expression of conjugal love is a splendid contribution, for it should induce Christian parents and teachers to undertake a sincere, searching reappraisal of their present negative approaches. Judging from their past records, this expectation or hope may appear overly optimistic, if not utterly naïve. Unaccustomed to taking a positive view of sex and confronted with rapid, extensive change affecting all aspects of life, contemporary Christian parents appear about as uncertain and confused as their children. Yet it should be obvious that Christian beliefs relating to marriage and the family can remain relevant only to the extent that they are formally conceptualized as values that "make sense" of the total reality of human sexuality, are adequately institutionalized in appropriate social standards and behavioral patterns, and are effectively internalized by youth through a form of consistent, supportive parental guidance, instruction, and training that not only informs but engenders affective commitment.

By way of conclusion, it may be well to note that although the Council was not able to deal with several key issues seriously troubling the consciences of many of the faithful, its pronouncements do reflect a refreshing awareness of these problems, and to a considerable extent, enlarge the framework of value premises and facts within which acceptable solutions must be found. Moreover, in their selection both of terms and areas of concern the Council Fathers showed their willingness to come to grips with the complex, multi-faceted reality we know as marriage and family. For as a total sharing of the whole of life, marriage is both "covenant" and "community" at the same time. As a union of love involving what is chosen, it is covenant; as a mysterious two-in-one-flesh procreative unity involving a unique givenness it is community. Among different family systems, as well as among individual marriages, primary concern may be placed on either covenant or community, on what is chosen or what is given; but both are involved in every marriage, and any authentic theology of marriage must give adequate consideration to both.

CHAPTER VI

CHRISTIAN CULTURE AND EDUCATION

Dr. George Shuster

"I don't want to ride in a car that goes so fast," an elderly African said in response to an invitation. "I'm afraid my spirit might get left behind." Perhaps a comparable anxiety, at a deeper but still cognate level of concern, was in the minds of the Council Fathers who endorsed those sections of the *Pastoral Constitution on the Church in the Modern World* which deal with education and culture. Manifestly the preservation and development of cultural values have been influenced in our time by forces of a magnitude and diversity probably unparalleled in the history of man. "Probably" seems an appropriate word because we are at present so overwhelmed by the rate of change that we may be unable to sense as clearly as the Council did what might be called the condition of permanence in the cultural life. Doubtless this condition of permanence was easier to manage during some previous eras of rapid shifting of the human dimension, for instance the period of mass migration to the United States. The many millions who passed through Ellis Island certainly found their experiences and their circumstances startlingly strange, but at the same time most of them seem to have vowed to preserve what they considered the abiding values of their cultural traditions.

For us the forces of change have come from so many directions with such speed and impact that almost no one has had a chance to list them in anything resembling a rational order, let alone analyze or understand them. In what now follows by way of comment on how Vatican II drew conclusions from its appraisal of them, no reference will be made to discussions which took place formally or informally prior to the endorsement of the document. These were interesting and upon occasion significant. But for better or for worse, only the naked text is before us.

It seems to me that the Council identified five kinds of cultural change:

First, the demonstrated efficiency and range of scientific thinking, which indeed has come to seem to many the only form in which a valid conceptualization of knowledge can take place.

Second, the tremendous social effect of technological management, based on the invention and exploitation of new means of mechanizing labor and movement.

Third, the resulting conflict between "fully developed" and more "primitive" cultures, both of which terms are used in the context of value judgments which may be superficial and time-bound.

Fourth, the growth of an attitude of mind to which the generic adjective "atheistic" may be attached — an attitude which in its simplest formulation takes it for granted that since man has solved problems of almost cosmic magnitude — an achievement which the *Constitution* candidly recognizes — without any discernible help from God or his spokesmen on earth, there is no longer a compelling reason for taking him or them into serious account.

Fifth, vastly increased participation in cultural goods and activities on a worldwide basis indicates that illiteracy and in a wider sense ignorance can be eradicated and replaced by ability to take part in the general cultural life of mankind.

What one is deeply impressed by in the first instance is the Council's ready acceptance of these changes as forming the framework within which the mission of the Church must henceforth be carried on. Some of us might have anticipated a sprinkle of anathemas, perhaps phrased more in the style of the London *Times* than of *Pravda* or even, let us say, *Ramparts* or the *Wanderer*. But there is none of that, though to be sure the *Constitution* does point to certain "dangers" and counsel avoidance of them. If one compares this *Constitution* with the two volumes of the Proceedings of the Eucharistic Congress which convened in Munich during 1960, ecumenical and contemporary in spirit though much of which was said there happened to be, one is quite literally astonished by the change in tone and temper. What had taken place is of course indicated by the following sentence in the Preface:

> . . . this Council can provide no more eloquent proof of solidarity with the whole human family with which it is bound up, as well as its respect and love for that family, than by engaging with it in conversation about these various problems.

How shall we picture for ourselves the part to be taken by the Church in the drama of enfolding cultural conversation? It may serve a useful purpose to consider briefly some of the memorable, now historical efforts to surmount what has so often been called the "ghetto mentality" of post-Tridentine Catholics. I believe that these were primarily three in number, although, to be sure, if the theme were broadened to include socio-political discussion major stress would have to be placed on the German experience of the post-Ketteler period. In the order of chronology, the three were these: first, the fruits of the Oxford Movement and of Newman's conversion, to which may be added the impact of the *Rambler* and the *Dublin Review* as well as the writings of Friedrich von Hügel; second, the growth of the University of Louvain and the coming into being by reason of Cardinal Mercier's initiative of a vigorous, though relatively abortive, ecumenical movement; and third, the *nouvelle théologie*, long associated by men of my generation with the *Nouvelle Revue théologique* which the Jesuits edited at Liége and which, it may be noted in passing, was not wholly without influence in the United States. All of these had their fruition in the *Constitution*, though not unnaturally the presence at the Council of the Cardinal Archbishop of Malines and of the great French theologians who had for so long a time served by standing and waiting most directly affected the outcome. No writing done in the pre-Conciliar period dealt more perceptively with the relationships between humanistic culture and theology than did that of Jacques Maritain. His deeply perceptive comment on human dignity and on pluralism is particularly memorable. But unfortunately there is little to indicate that these writings had any marked influence on those most responsible for the chapter of the *Constitution* under discussion here.

To return to the question just asked. The answers depend on certain assumptions clearly stated. These are that the Church is divinely commissioned to show men the way to salvation through Jesus Christ, that every human person possesses a dignity which is to be considered inviolate, and that each of us can tragically mar that dignity as incarnate in oneself or incarnate in others. These are the basic axioms from which the reasoning proceeds.

The answers given are:

First, the fact that Christians acknowledge that life on this earth is a pilgrimage "in no way decreases but actually increases the weight of their obligation to work with all men in constructing a more human world."[1]

Second, intellectual and ethical civility is (as Newman so stoutly insisted) an aid to the "freedom from bondage" to evil inclinations which is properly the gift of the Holy Spirit.

Third, the scientific component of contemporary culture may so absorb men's attention that they will tend to be disinterested in or "agnostic about everything else." Nevertheless, science fosters important natural virtues, such as "strict fidelity to truth," and is therefore a handmaiden, when properly understood, to the Church's quest for man's salvation.

Fourth, the Church, active in many disparate cultures and

---

[1] Confer the writing of Teilhard de Chardin.

showing great ability to accommodate itself to what is best and most distinctive about them, as its liturgy also indicates, has an opportunity to foster a mutual enrichment of cultures.

Fifth, the "two orders of knowledge," which are faith and reason, must not (the Council here reiterated and amplified the language of the first Vatican Council) lead to disregard "of the autonomy of each other." Indeed, in both cases "let it be recognized that all the faithful, clerical and lay, possess a lawful freedom of inquiry and of thought, and the freedom to express their minds humbly and courageously about those matters in which they possess competence."

Sixth, every human being has a right to profit by the fruits of culture and should be assisted in fostering his ability to exercise it. The duty of a Catholic Christian is positive in the sense, for example, that he should help to wipe out as rapidly as possible the scourge of illiteracy, and negative in the sense that he must abhor discrimination "on the grounds of race, sex, nationality, religion, or social conditions."

So ringing and indeed unprecedented is the endorsement of the right of the scholar to seek truth and to present his findings, subject only to criticism of his competence, that not a few have found it relatively astonishing. Although *aggiornamento* certainly was necessary in order to give this teaching its honored place in a Conciliar declaration, it will not seem very strange even to anyone who has, as I do, only a superficial acquaintance with the thought of St. Thomas. Nevertheless, the context in which this freedom is now placed — a context which the *Constitution* describes with remarkable clarity and completeness — is quite different from any that could have suggested itself to the Angelic Doctor; and it is this difference which lies at the root of the perturbation which not a few feel when brought face to face with the fact that even the *nouvelle théologie* of some years ago is now only partially new. We need not blind ourselves to the probability that a measure of anxiety exists particularly in the United States, where until very recently the training provided in seminaries and religious houses generally was conventional, and where conversation even between priests and Catholic layfolk educated differently has been at best no more than sporadic.

Normally, a Catholic of whatever status in religion has had little opportunity to realize how secular the prevailing culture of the West has become. He knows, of course, that there is more laxity in the area of sexual morality, that the movies and the theater are less wholesome and decent, and that there has been some kind of conflict between theology and science. But that there are many prominent intellectuals and makers of public opinion for whom religion has ceased to be in any genuine sense significant is a fact he can have had little opportunity to discover. As a product of Catholic schooling he might often assume that the Thomistic philosophy provided a solid, dependable jointure of reason and faith. But he cannot be expected to realize that in American philosophy as a whole pragmatism virtually ceased to develop just at the point where its concern with theism seemed likely to prove creative and fruitful or that the several varieties of logical positivism — not all of which were, as Warren Weaver has effectively contended, necessarily anti-religious — were rather suddenly merged in forms of analysis for analysis' sake, in order, it appears, belatedly to get rid of Hegel. Nor could he easily realize that when much Protestant thinking, that of John Dewey for example, veered from Hegelianism to determinism something fateful had happened which would leave a mark temporarily indelible on the American mind.

A comparable development had taken place earlier in Europe, and with it important essays as well as the later correspondence of Newman were devoted either in terms of recognition or of prediction. The thoughtful Catholic scholar of the mid-twentieth century could not avoid seeing that he was living in a diaspora — that the older Catholic peoples of Europe had to a very great and tragic extent lost their faith, except sometimes an elementary form of conformism. For this not only social injustice was responsible, or a too long continued identification

of the Church with repression. Among the major causes were
certainly a sequence of ideologies nearly all of which were
rooted in highly individualistic, rebellious philosophies. The
variants of determinism have been many and variously de-
structive — the determinisms of the class struggle, of race, of
the survival of the strong. Yet it must be said candidly that all
these things could not have decimated Christendom so savagely
had it not been for the rise of the conviction that the problem
of evil is beyond solution. It was the powerlessness of the individual in the face of tyranny which was so awesome and
awful, so shattering and unnerving an experience. Early Christians were unnerved by it too, as the Book of the Apocalypse
bears witness. But men of an era contemporary with our own
had doubtless lived too comfortably in the green pastures of a
Christendom triumphant over its enemies. That this kind of
victory, a welcome gift though it doubtless was, could be considered identical with the Savior's vanquishing of the world, as
he defined the world, was a delusion. Too many in the Church
thought that if they could somehow cling to the trappings of
the Constantinian victory, however tattered, peace would come
to them in the end. That is probably why there was no ringing
protest against Auschwitz. And this is why Hitler could steadily
draw a noose round the throat of the Church, which indeed
might well have strangled it.

Does it not upon occasion seem that the Church in the United
States has been too optimistic in another sense? It may still
be too proudly conscious of its strength. This, of course, we
should not disparage. The strength has sound roots. But the
spiritual landscape is not dotted with regrettable structures like
the Shrine of the Immaculate Conception or even of beautiful
ones like the Church of St. John's Abbey. It stretches out to
life over a bridge of the bones of saints.

Here, then, is the Council, instead of being dizzy and ap-
palled, as Newman sometimes was, by what could be seen in a
glance backwards over the totalitarian years, or discerned from
what Western culture was currently saying about itself, calling

out not from safe towers or embattlements, but from a place in the streets. "Let us talk to a world without a home about its potential everlasting dwelling in God's bosom. We, the little flock, the *pucillis grex,* mindful of our relationship with the early Christian family, will enter into conversation with the whole of humankind. And to what purpose? Because it has been given to us to show the world the way to salvation through Christ Jesus not merely for the sake of the hereafter, but for the sake also of the here and now. Like Paul we know neither bondsmen nor freemen, we are not afraid of the strength of Athens or the forums of Rome." You may answer that a stout heart is called for, but the Council began this *Constitution* with the word, *Gaudium,* which means joy. To leave the walled towns, the barbed wire, and the palisades behind, and go out to share with all the people, talk with each and everyone of them, do with all of them the things which so badly need to be done! What a young Church this must be, and may God grant that the hearts of the young can accept the challenge.

Lest you think that the authors of the *Constitution* went on some kind of binge, bear in mind that something marvelously akin to Pentecost is always taking place — some manifestation of the life of the *Logos* that is in seed when not in flower. One has to look and listen. Of this we have had no more awesome demonstration than that provided by Jewish women in the pre-Hitler time whose intuitions of the fate which evil had in store for the people from whom they were sprung seem upon reflection so breathtakingly startling. There were not a few and I shall name only four — Simone Weil, Elizabeth-Lasker-Schu-eler, Edith Stein, Raissa Maritain. On the one hand their sense of impending doom was almost as overpowering as Mary's at the moment of surmisal (of what the Germans so wonder-fully call *Ahnung*) of what would befall her Son. They were like the woman who bore the veil on which the Lord Jesus dried his face. Nothing is deeper in the mystery of the Incarnation than the fact that whatever proneness to evil stirs in the heart of man cannot rise to greater heights than did the hatred

of the Divine Good for patriotic and therefore worldly reasons
in the narrow framework of Palestinian civilization. But, quite
astonishing this, the women of whom I have spoken came down
strange ways to the feet of God. Simone Weil is the most
inspiring fashioner of prayers in our time, and Elizabeth Las-
ker-Schueler one of that time's most haunting religious poets.

Right under our noses another kind of stirring has been
taking place. Young people on campuses or off may get fright-
fully fed up on courses in theology. Doubtless they should
manifest a greater interest in a treatise on the trinity, but they
would perversely rather read *The Portrait of the Artist as a
Young Man*. But watch them with CILA in the country of pov-
erty-glutted mountains east of Santiago. See them with the
Peace Corps in the slums of Lima. Observe them at work in
the decaying cities of this country. There the "people of God"
come alive for them, the thought of Christ is real, the vision
of a young Church is born, in which everyone — priests, religious, laymen and laywomen — find religion relevant.

It is extremely difficult to comment on the implications of
this "coming alive." The creative individual can, of course, find
his way. He can, like a young North American friend of mine,
throw himself fully into the life struggle of slum dwellers in
Colombia, or work for the starving people of Kerala, India.
But how do all the societies and sodalities, the councils and
fraternities, which we have so laboriously established to serve
parishes or ward off "secular" influences, suddenly find the key
to cooperating with international liberating efforts, for instance,
UNESCO and the UN, or discover how to face the world as it
would be if delegates from the People's Republic of China
suddenly showed up in New York (as they probably will)? What
shall these organizations do? Whatever the answer is, they will
need a whale of a lot of preparation. We have spent decades
conditioning them one way. It is to be doubted that six months
will suffice the other way round. The Holy Family Guild of St.
Anselm's will not only undertake to supply flowers for the altar
but will be encouraged to take a deep, sincere interest in Chris-

tian and Catholic activities elsewhere in the world.

When one thinks of these things and many more besides, the almost aggressive affirmations of the *Constitution* seem to become not flags but lanterns. Souls are to be saved, for time and the timelessness beyond it, within the setting of an industrial and technological culture. The fact that this is an age of machines, chemistry, engineering, medical advance, psychiatric care, did not becloud the outlook of the Fathers or unsteady their hands. They seem not to have worried about whether radioactive waste is harder to get rid of than the dung in cow barns. Their eyes were on the changes which will also bring improvement if we know what to do and do it. There is no dismal science in the *Constitution*. Ignorance, disease, undernourishment can be banished.

Nonetheless, at this point I find a sizeable blank page in this *Constitution*. If Catholic Christians are on the one hand to engage in discussion with the whole human family, and on the other hand to exercise leadership in bringing about some sort of equalization of access to cultural goods, they cannot fragmentize their efforts. They must have centers in which they can deepen their awareness of major issues, engage in fruitful conversation among themselves before they take on the rest of the world, and learn not only how to get their feet wet but how to swim under water. Yet it is precisely here that the Council left an almost blank page. Obviously, the list of such centers must include the universities, for they are the primary scenes of modern cultural confrontation.

This one does not have to prove. *Pacem in terris* set an example by taking it for granted. Naturally, we do not mean that henceforth fruitful dialogue between the people of God and the society in which it exists is to take place in academic language only. Even the world's poor will talk to one another about suffering, sacrifice, joy, longing, kindness, need. Their conversation will run the gamut of the beatitudes and the seven capital sins. Still, it is a world of the abstract intelligence which we and they inhabit; and the burning question is, where shall the

Christian formation of that intelligence begin? This is a con-
undrum which the Council seems not to have taken sufficiently
into account. To be sure, education must be viewed in a much
broader context, and this becomes clear if one reads the *Constitution* as a whole, and does not concentrate only on culture as
we are doing here.

First, there is the Catholic university. That there are highly
important differences between the mold in which it was originally cast, and in which it is still to some extent confined by
canonical regulations, and the mode of institutionalized free
conversation which the Fathers so confidently proclaimed, seems
quite clear. The original intention certainly was to provide in
the form of higher education an instrumentality through which
the teaching authority of the Church was to manifest itself. Perhaps one may say not unfairly that what had been visualized
was instruction and not research. The soundness of the theological doctrine expounded was to be assured by a professional
oath of fidelity to the *Magisterium*. Philosophy was to be Thomistic, with minor deviations permitted to religious orders having
traditions of their own. Colleges of medicine and law were to
foster the Christian ethic pertinent to these professions. And
the basic humanistic concern was to be with "Christian culture."

Already in present practice these restrictions have for all
practical purposes been removed or curtailed, sometimes perhaps too hastily and headily. Surely, it would be rather odd if
a young man desiring to study the Christian cultural tradition
would have to matriculate in the University of Chicago, or a
young lady, eager to steep herself in Christian Platonism,
could do no better than try to worm her way into the male
fortress of Princeton. Curiously enough, though this is not yet
quite the case, it almost is. Philosophers one consults indicate
that the number of distinguished Thomists is small. Personalism,
existentialism, and the philosophy of science are almost as un-
avoidable on Catholic campuses as are glimpses of the clergy.
And though I am a rank amateur in theological matters, it ap-
ears to be true that the average university theologian would

be hard put to answer the question, to precisely what would an oath bind me, apart from basic and inviolate dogma?

Second, the secular university may be seen as an institution in which Catholic scholarship and commitment are to manifest themselves in the general cultural conversation. Several patterns have emerged: that of the German university, with a Catholic faculty of theology; that of Oxford, with its center serving general Catholic intellectual interests and activities; that of the University of Toronto, having a separate and indeed distinctive Catholic college; and that of a secular university in the United States, offering a "pluralistic" solution of the religious "problem" and sometimes even making it possible to take courses in religion for credit. It is apparent that all of these owe their existence to an amalgam of pastoral and academic concern. But though their disparateness is a sign of life, it is certainly not a proof that the spirit which the *Constitution* would infuse into the family of God will necessarily find the given institutional base everything which could be desired. The situation obviously suggests a need for careful study.

The question whether a Catholic university should exist at all unless it has a clearly defined part to play in the kind of world which the Council has mapped out cannot be answered until the reasons for having such a university have been carefully formulated and discussed. Personally I am sure they can be, but they will be quite different from those which would have seemed appropriate a hundred years ago. They will be good reasons if in the broad overall university community they seem liberating and not obscurantist. Thus one thinks that an excellent case for a law school in a Catholic university can be made, on the ground that the social ethic it professes, being that of the Second Vatican Council, will train young men and women for service in the kind of world which must come to be if the world is to exist at all. Insofar as the United States is concerned, the Catholic university has been based on the belief of the Catholic people that every institution committed to Christ and his Church was necessarily a good thing. This belief will persist, but the commitment must be to the Christian mission of the future and not to the Christian mission of the past.

Although the problem just referred to can be summed up as unfinished business, there can be little doubt, thank God, that by reason of the *Constitution* the cultural mission of the Church has been given a charter by which it can live if the language becomes more than static print. The Church, whose missionary effort brought it during many centuries into loving and healing association with many cultures, so that its gift of adaptation far exceeds that of any other form of society, now has a wonderful mission of reconciliation not merely between nation and nation, or between culture and culture, but also and perhaps especially between the older rural social order and the emerging products of technological change. True enough, the people of God have sometimes slept or, what is worse, had bad dreams. But a great stirring seems to be taking place. Only we must not think (and of course you will not) that we now have the solutions for all problems. The *Constitution* wrote the first page in a new book. It will take a long time until the last page has been written.

CHAPTER VII

THE COUNCIL AND ECONOMIC LIFE

Dr. John Joseph Murphy

I

An evaluation of the importance of the socioeconomic pronouncements of the Second Vatican Council produces something
of a paradox. On the one hand, they are primarily reiterations
of positions already put forth in the great social encyclicals,
especially those of Pope John XXIII. On the other hand, inasmuch as no previous council saw fit to address itself to such
"mundane" issues, the Second Vatican Council, in just repeat-
ing the Church's socioeconomic positions, gives to these teachings a universal measure of importance that no one can now
deny. Thus while offering nothing truly new in doctrine, the
socioeconomic pronouncements of Vatican II, especially those
contained in the *Constitution on the Church in the Modern
World,* offer something truly new in emphasis.

My task is to analyze the main principles set forth in these
pronouncements[1] and to indicate some of the implications of
these principles given the facts of mid-twentieth century life.
The analysis is from the perspective of a social scientist and it

---

[1] The analysis in this paper proceeds on the assumption that the economic doctrines enunciated at the Second Vatican Council are one with
those put forth by Pope John in his encyclicals *Mater et Magistra* and
Pacem in Terris. The consistent references in the *Constitution on the
Church in the Modern World* to Pope John's statements indicate the
continuity that the Council Fathers saw between their positions and
those of Pope John.

has as its primary objective the directive of Pope John that the Church's teachings must be applied to the situation that *actually* exists (MeM, 236).[2]

I will proceed in four parts. First, I will develop the general economic[3] propositions that the Council Fathers put forth. Second, I will indicate the approach of the Council to three specific economic questions. Third, I will outline, for selected economic issues, directions in which the conciliar teachings might be fruitfully developed. Finally, I will provide a brief summary of the meaning for the modern world of the economic pronouncements of Vatican II.

II

At the heart of the Council's position on economic issues is the recognition that the "signs of the times" indicate that the modern world is "passing through a new stage of history" (CMW, 4). In this new stage man is caught up in a process of continuous change that, besides exposing him to the constant emergence of new artifacts and new technological devices, involves him in a new perception of the world he lives in. Mankind, the Council Fathers observe, has passed "from a rather static concept of reality to a more dynamic, evolutionary one" (CMW, 5).

This new perception of his total ecological situation leads man into "true" social and cultural transformations that have important repercussions on his religious life as well as on his material life (CMW, 4). With this new perspective, man is

---

[2] Instead of using footnotes, references to the main documents analyzed will be given in parentheses in the text using the abbreviations "CMW" for the *Constitution on the Church in the Modern World*, "MeM" for *Mater et Magistra*, and "PiT" for *Pacem in Terris*. The figure given after each abbreviation will be the appropriate paragraph number. For direct quotations, the author has relied upon the translations contained in Walter M. Abbott. S.J., gen. ed., *The Documents of Vatican II* (New York: America Press and others, 1966), and the National Catholic Welfare Conference's editions of the encyclicals.

[3] I will use the term "economic" instead of "socioeconomic" inasmuch as the main tenor of my paper concerns economic issues. I use the term, however, in its broadest sense.

rejecting such traditional concepts as a fixed state in life or a passive resignation to fate, and he is replacing them with a firm belief that it is within his own ability to control his material progress. Given this belief, modern man, when he is denied such progress or when he does not share justly in the progress that is achieved, becomes impatient and tends to seek redress in ways that are often contrary to those that will truly aid him in developing his total self.

In order to avoid such ill-advised solutions to the aspirations that almost all men now hold, it is necessary that correct decisions be made concerning the economic system, both national and international (CMW, 60). These decisions must begin with "new efforts of analysis and synthesis" (CMW, 5), a task that permeates the document that the Second Vatican Council addresses to "the whole of humanity" (CMW, 2).

In the economic sphere the Council sees these correct decisions as leading to optimum rates of growth, stability, and equitable distribution. "There must be available to all men," the Council Fathers write, "everything necessary for leading a life truly human;" and they list among these necessities such economic factors as food, clothing, shelter, the right to choose a state of life freely, the right to education, and the right to employment (CMW, 25).[4] Later they make quite clear how such necessities can be made available to all men: "technical progress must be fostered, along with a spirit of initiative, an eagerness to create and expand enterprises, the adaptation of methods of production, and the strenuous efforts of all who engage in production — in a word, all the elements making for such development" (CMW, 64). This emphasis upon preconditions for eco-

---

[4] Pope John was even more explicit about the general economic factors that all men need and have a right to obtain: "Every man has the right to life, to bodily integrity, and to the means which are necessary and suitable for the proper development of life. These means are primarily food, clothing, shelter, rest, medical care, and finally the necessary social services.

"Therefore, a human being also has the right to security in cases of sickness, inability to work, widowhood, old age, unemployment, or in any other case in which he is deprived of the means of subsistence through no fault of his own." (PiT, 11)

nomic growth follows Pope John's explicit notations that in most cases the causes of poverty "are to be found in the primitive and state of the economy," that the proper remedy of this condition is through increased investment in human and physical capital (MeM, 163).

An economist may be forgiven for seeing in these statements the essence of the "Protestant Ethic" thesis that Max Weber put forth fifty years ago. This is not to suggest, however, that the Church Fathers have simply baptized in this ecumenical age the economic thought of the Calvinist and Lutheran dissenters, for they go well beyond a simple achievement motivation-abstentious consumption doctrine to an expression of the very positive part that conscious human decision-making on both the individual and the societal level must play in order to accomplish the ends of economic growth, stability, and justice. And while they do not equate economic success with holiness, they do see in basic economic progress an essential condition for the complete spiritual fulfillment of the average man. To the churchmen who formed Vatican II, when the average man is in extreme poverty, he is less than human and he is, therefore, not fully capable of rising to his destiny with God (CMW, 31).

The Council Fathers see the way out of this poverty to be through the discovery and utilization of the laws that an economic system by its nature is endowed with. In a passage that totally refutes the old shibboleth of a dichotomy between science and religion, the Council Fathers place on the social scientist the obligation of deciphering, putting to use, and regulating, "in accord with moral norms," the economic environment and thereby providing the setting for earthly progress that will better order human society (CMW, 36). The fulfillment of this task, they go on to proclaim, "is of vital concern to the kingdom of God" (CMW, 39).

This is not just a willingness to allow economic growth to occur; it is a positive desire to foster it. This does not make the Council Fathers growth advocates simply for the sake of growth, as is often the case with modern economists. Nor does it make the Fathers growth advocates for the sake of increasing national power, as is the case with so many in both developed and developing countries. The Council Fathers desire economic growth because they have as the focal point of their economic concern man as an individual. Economic growth is good because man himself, "whole and entire, body and soul, heart and conscience, mind and will," requires it in order to fulfill his destiny (CMW, 3).[5]

If economic growth is necessary for man to fulfill himself in this new evolutionary world, so are stability and equity in the economic system. The Council Fathers recognize that most men support themselves and their families by the earnings they derive from contributing their labor to the productive process, and the Fathers therefore argue that it is of the highest priority to provide such individuals with work opportunities at all times. "It is the duty of society," they state, "according to the circumstances prevailing in it, and in keeping with its proper role, to help its citizens find opportunities for adequate employment" (CMW, 67). This is particularly true in this world of technological change, where "care must be taken that sufficient and suitable work can be obtained, along with appropriate technical and professional formation" (CMW, 66). This call for continuous training and retraining as the techniques of the modern economic system become more sophisticated and complex sounds very familiar to anyone who has dealt with the current problems of structural unemployment in the United States.

The Council Fathers are even more concerned, as the language they use shows, with inequitable distribution of what is produced, although they see the obvious connection between

---

[5] The emphasis upon the "Dignity of the Human Person," as the first chapter of CMW is entitled, is what differentiates Catholic social thought from that of many other reform movements that advocate similar programs. By consistently emphasizing the inviolable rights of the individual, the Church has avoided sliding into the fallacy of the greatest good for the greatest number regardless of the cost to the remainder of the population, a doctrine that has debased many otherwise worthwhile movements of modern times.

full employment of a skilled labor force and the equity of distribution. In definitive terms they judge: "excessive economic and social differences between members of the one human family or population groups cause scandal, and militate against social justice, equity, and the dignity of the human person, as well as social and international peace" (CMW, 29). In the light of such a statement no Catholic will be able to argue against the *principle* of "wars on poverty" at home or abroad.[6]

The Council, like Pope John before it, is not content simply to condemn excessive unemployment or excessive differences in income but goes on to state that it is a particular responsibility of governments, national and international, to take action in these areas for the sake of the common good. Pope John was most explicit in this regard. He saw in the recent advances in science and technology "additional reasons why, to a greater extent than heretofore, it is within the power of public authorities to reduce imbalances, whether these be between various sectors of economic life, or between different regions of the same nation, or even between different peoples of the world as a whole" (MeM, 54). The Council Fathers repeat in only slightly different words this same position as they note that government intervention is necessary in order to bring "about conditions more likely to help citizens and groups freely attain to complete human fulfillment with greater effect" (CMW, 75).

The emphasis in the documents of Vatican II on the positive function that governments should play in directing economic affairs is consistent with the whole line of Catholic socioeconomic thought. In words similar to those used by Pope Leo XIII in the nineteenth century, the Council condemns unregulated *laissez faire* as belonging to those "theories which obstruct . . . necessary reforms in the name of a false liberty." But

---

[6] Pope John was equally emphatic. "The economic prosperity of any people is to be assessed not so much from the sum total of goods and wealth possessed as from the distribution of goods according to norms of justice, so that everyone in the community can develop and perfect himself. For this, after all, is the end toward which all economic activity of a community is by nature ordered" (MeM, 74).

because the Council is not caught in the trap of those who see only two possible economic systems — one with no government or one with all government — it as readily condemns those economic systems that "subordinate the basic rights of individual persons and groups to the collective organization of production" (CMW, 65). What the Council envisions is an economic system that falls between these two extremes, a system wherein the state performs a positive function that not only does not constrain human freedom but actually enlarges it.

One of the bases for advocating such a mixed economic system is in the Council's acceptance of Pope John's recognition of the increased "socialization" that marks modern industrialized societies. There is no need to elaborate on how this term was misunderstood when it appeared in the initial English translations of *Mater et Magistra*[7] beyond wondering why people long exposed to "outer directed individuals," "organization men," "power elites," and modern suburban living could be bothered by papal recognition of the fact that "one of the principal characteristics of our time is . . . a daily more complex interdependence of citizens" (MeM, 59).

The Council Fathers recognize that this growing interdependence brings with it "dangers," but they are not as terrified as many American and English social critics who see in this expansion of man's historic tendency to group action the destruction of the species. Instead, the Council Fathers find in increased socialization "many advantages with respect to consolidating and increasing the qualities of the human person and safeguarding his rights" (CMW, 25). They believe this can be accomplished if the state uses the increased socialization as a framework for providing increased unity in the economic system (CMW, 42).

The framework that the Council Fathers have in mind is the one Pope John enunciated. It is one that free men, acting in con-

---

[7] The misunderstanding was so great that later English translations shied away from the word "socialization." The *Constitution on the Church in the Modern World* no longer makes this possible.

formity with their nature, create (MeM, 63). Thus it is not the result of historical determinism nor is it a natural equilibrium state. It is, instead, one that is brought into existence through free, conscious, human decisions that have as their objective the establishment of a state of economic activity that provides optimum welfare for all citizens (MeM, 64). Such a state is one wherein each action is the responsibility of the appropriate body (MeM, 65). This reaffirmation of the principle of subsidarity is no mere tautological statement but frames clearly the essence of the modern mixed economy whose basic structure implies granting to whatever component can most efficiently achieve a given objective the right and duty of carrying out the operation. This can be done, as Pope John wrote, only if the state keeps in balance: "The freedom of individual citizens and groups of citizens to act autonomously, while cooperating one with the other," and "the activity of the State whereby the undertakings of private individuals and groups are suitably regulated and fostered" (MeM, 66).

III

In the jargon of the economist, the economic system the Council Fathers outline is one that is in an equilibrium growth pattern, that maintains as fully an employed economy as possible, and that distributes the output of the economy in the most equitable, yet efficient, manner. This is not a utopian scheme, for the Council Fathers recognize that in a dynamic, evolutionary system some unemployment will occur because some imbalances are necessary. They also recognize that men possess different talents and contribute in different ways to the economic process and that inasmuch as the economic process does have its own laws it is necessary to remunerate different labor in different amounts. But within these limitations they advocate — as many welfare economists also advocate — that the systems be structured so as to minimize human discomforts and inequalities. For a modern economy, they argue, such a structure uses private initiative as its main force, group action as its main means, and positive government direction as its main regulator. And they interpret such an equilibrium economic system to be one that embraces all of the economies of the world and not just the economy of a given nation state.

The statements of Pope John and of the Council are general outlines and do not contain detailed explanations of how balanced economies on the national or international level are to be achieved. They do comment, however, upon some specific problems that will have to be resolved before such balanced economic systems can become operative. Among the more important of these problems are those that concern the relation between the rate of population growth and the rate of economic growth, sectoral imbalances within nations, and sectoral imbalances among nations. It is to these three issues that this paper now turns.

Because most commentators became caught up in the emotional or theological nature of the moral aspects of the means of limiting births, they failed to give adequate recognition to the significance of what the *Pastoral Constitution on the Church in the Modern World* did say about the relation between family size and economic welfare. Early in this *Constitution*, the Council Fathers observe that one aspect of the revolution that modern man is passing through involves the human race in "giving ever-increasing thought to forecasting and regulating its own population growth" (CMW, 4). This is said neither in approval nor disapproval but simply as a fact. Later, when they turn to more explicit comments on the population question, they provide the economic basis of this fact and recognize this basis as a relevant consideration in the determination by married couples of the size of their family.

They begin by noting that there exist "those peoples who, in addition to many other problems, are today often enough burdened in a special way with the difficulties stemming from a rapid population growth" (CMW, 87). While they advocate that international aid be forthcoming to mitigate this problem and while they expressly condemn any direct grovernment intervention that has as its objective the radical reduction of population growth, the Council Fathers place their main stress upon the responsibility that resides with parents: "The question of how many children should be born belongs to the honest judgment of parents." This "honest judgment," the Council goes on to state, requires "a rightly formed conscience" that "respects the divine law and *takes account of circumstances and the times*" (CMW, 87, emphasis added).

Now while I do not wish to violate the Council's warning against appropriating the Church's authority for his opinion (CMW, 43), as an economist I find it difficult not to interpret the above-emphasized words in the context of the detailed and explicit notations that the Council Fathers earlier provide on how degrading poverty is to the fulfillment of each man's destiny. And in a document that emphasizes the revolutionary, evolutionary nature of the times and that goes on to emphasize that economic advancement is one of the key aspects of this revolutionary period, the notice that parents should consider the "circumstances and the times" implies to me that responsible parenthood includes considering the common good of the nation and the international community. To avoid what has become a common erroneous evaluation of the position just stated, I would like to emphasize that I am not implying that the Council said anything about the moral aspects of mechanisms for limiting the size of families. This, as the Church Fathers consistently made clear, is left up to the Papal Commission and to the Holy Father. What the Council did do was to recognize that a direct relation exists between population growth and poverty and that it is incumbent that people be well-informed about the mundane as well as the religious side of such an issue and that when so informed they act responsibly.

Such a balanced economic system requires that the various economic and geographic sectors receive equitable compensation for what they contribute. This is not the balanced growth thesis of modern development economists, but a balanced system thesis that is growth oriented and that requires that society take

specific actions to correct income differential abuses.[8] Among
the specific actions the Council recommends are agricultural
price protection ("by methods worked out by economic experts,"
as Pope John phrased it. MeM, 137), free labor unions, some
form of property ownership, the fostering of small businesses
and cooperative enterprises (MeM, 85 ff.), and the active participation of all in some control over the general direction that
the economic system takes. But above all the Council Fathers
place the development of human resources as *the* way to affect
major and equitable changes in any economic system; and they
place the utilization of such labor with the most advanced technology as the best mechanism for achieving such development.

The words which the Council Fathers direct against the inequalities that exist among nations convey an even deeper
anguish than those that refer to inequalities within nations. This
sincere concern with international relations marks, as it does the
great documents issued by Pope John and Pope Paul, the universal nature of the Church's concern and confirms the sincerity
of the appeals to "all men of good will" (PiT) and to "the whole
of humanity" (CMW, 2). The world, the Council Fathers warn,
must take those steps necessary to eliminate the inequities that
exist between developed and developing nations. Among the more
important of these steps is increased "human and financial assistance" and a significant restructuring of the procedures of
international trade (CMW, 85). And while the Council condemns that type of intervention that we in the West associate
with communist international subversion, it must be remembered
that the Council equally condemns "excessive desire for profit."

Above all, the Council sees the solution of the disparities that
exist at the international level in simultaneous action. At the
national level actions must be instituted to use to their maximum
efficiency the resources available. At the international level "adequate organizations . . . for fostering and harmonizing inter-

---

[8] Farmers, in particular, are noted as being in danger of becoming or
remaining "lower-class citizens." Similar warnings are given concerning
those who have migrated and those who are disposed of by automation
(CMW, 66).

national trade" must be established. This recognition of the necessity of cooperation at all levels in the international community includes a call for regulation of the international economy which, when "combined with technical, cultural, and financial help, ought to afford the needed assistance to nations striving for progress, enabling them to achieve economic growth expeditiously" (CMW, 86).[9]

Although the Council does not cover in the same specifics that Pope John did issues relevant to this "most pressing question of our day" (MeM, 157), the documents of Vatican II leave no doubt that the Council Fathers also consider the necessity of narrowing the gap between rich lands and poor lands to be one of the prime tasks of our time.

IV

While the economic pronouncements of the Second Vatican Council concern some of the major problems that beset this modern world of change, they include neither all of the problems nor detailed prescriptions for the solution of those which they do consider. This, of course, is in line with the general nature of conciliar documents and it is why such teachings — regardless of how wise or insightful they may be — have an impact upon the world only to the extent that others pick up the general guidelines and develop them into more concrete positions. The true meaning of Vatican II, therefore, will be found in developments that are yet to come and it is with this in mind that I now turn to consider three questions that were not dealt with specifically in the documents of the Council: the place of national economic planning in the Church's general doctrines; the meaning of the Church's teaching on private property for a large enterprise economy; and the proper structure of the international economic community.

Since World War II almost all of the economies of the noncommunist world have undergone profound changes. Among all of these changes two stand out as of signal importance. One is

---

[9] Interestingly, it is at this point that the Council refers specifically to the principle of subsidiarity.

that in all economies the central government has been given the task of achieving the basic economic objectives of growth, stability, equitable distribution, and expanded economic opportunities. No longer is any major nation committed to a *laissez faire* philosophy; what now differentiates nations is the form of positive government policies that they invoke.

The second item of importance is that many nations have come to reach for these goals via some system of national planning. This planning is not of the type associated with the total control over the economy which either the Soviet Union or mainland China exercises and that the Council condemns. What has emerged in the non-communist world involves either trying to establish more precise long-run objectives for all major sectors (as is exemplified in the planning mechanisms of Western Europe), or trying to allocate very scarce resources and foreign exchange more efficiently in order to achieve a take-off into self-sustained economic growth. If either of these forms of planning can accomplish their basic objective of minimizing business cycle fluctuations or of increasing the per capita output, then they will also increase the freedom of the individual, as the Council observes greater economic stability and growth are capable of doing.

The antisocialism approach of Church pronouncements since the nineteenth century has left in the minds of many an equation between government attempts to regulate an economy and anti-Christian behavior. This has been especially true when the governmental efforts have involved "planning." Although the Church's condemnation of socialism is quite clear, it is also quite clear that the Church has equally condemned that state of affairs where the government has played no role whatsoever in directing the economy. The question raised, therefore, is whether government intervention through an avowed planning mechanism comes closer to the Church's traditional definition of socialism or her traditional definition of subsidiarity.

The Council's general notations about the necessity for the public authority intervening more and more today in order to bring "about conditions more likely to help citizens and groups freely attain to complete human fulfillment with greater effect," and its more specific notations concerning the role of public authorities in maintaining full employment or in increasing the rate of economic growth suggest that the answer is that a correctly structured national planning system falls legitimately within the subsidiarity boundaries of a correctly ordered economic system.

Such national planning mechanism obviously must not be used to deny to individuals that freedom which is theirs due to their nature, nor must planning be used to harm those institutions that are part of the traditional culture — unless such institutions are, themselves, detrimental to the achievement of the common good. The Council's statements on "the distribution of goods" make clear what the objectives of such a planning system must be (CMW, 70). After specifically noting that it may be either individuals, groups, or public authorities that make the decisions, the Council goes on to talk about "their serious obligation" of providing for a "decent life" for both those now living and those yet to come. This "serious obligation" entails establishing a "proper balance between the needs of present-day consumption, both individual and collective, and the necessity of distributing goods on behalf of the coming generation." A planning system with these objectives would seem to be one of those institutions that Pope John explicitly recognized; "It is requested again and again of public authorities responsible for the common good, that they intervene in a wide variety of economic affairs, and that, in a more extensive and organized way than heretofore, they adapt institutions, tasks, means, and procedures to this end" (MeM, 54).

Inasmuch as the relation between government interference in the economic system and private property are so common in the minds of Western educated individuals, it might not be completely fortuitous that the Council's statements on ownership and property should follow immediately upon those calling for a "proper balance" in the system. As Pope John XXIII did in

Mater et Magistra, the Council Fathers reaffirm how important it is for the complete fulfillment of the individual both in his personality and in his freedom that he have access to private property. But in contrast to pre-World War II statements, the longer portion of the Council's remarks on property have to do with the rights of public ownership, the social quality of property, and consequently the requirements that private property be correctly used for the economic welfare of the nation.[10]

The statements of the Council on private property can lead to three interpretations which may be, but are not necessarily, contradictory. First, the statements obviously reaffirm the right of individuals to own material goods, including the means of production. Second, the statements show that when such ownership is not being exercised to accomplish communal ends, the state not only can but must bring such ownership to an end. Finally, with all of the emphasis in other Council documents on the rapidity of change that is affecting the economic area, in the matter of private property the Council does not (nor did Pope John before it) consider in depth the meaning of private property when it takes the form of the modern corporate giant.

Traditionally the Church has taught that private property has specific advantages for these reasons: because man takes better care of what he is personally in charge of; because the management of goods by individuals achieves a better social order; and because peace is better guaranteed if everyone is satisfied with what he has. This traditional teaching must be recognized as being basically oriented to an agrarian-artisan economy and as less and less relevant to what Father Harbrecht has so appropriately called a "paraproprietal society."[11] The hiatus that this new society is creating is indicated in a passage in *Mater et Magistra* where Pope John called for widespread "private possession of such things as durable goods, homes, gardens, tools

---

[10] The most famous of these statements is the Council's recognition of the right to expropriate agricultural land that is "only moderately cultivated or lies completely idle for the sake of profit" (CMW, 71).

[11] Paul Harbrecht, S.J., *Pension Funds and Economic Power* (New York: The Twentieth Century Fund, 1959), Chap. 10.

requisite for artisan enterprises and family-type farms, investments in enterprises of medium or large size" (MeM, 115).[12] Herein the Pontiff equated the ownership of those goods one could control with the ownership of titles to enterprises that one normally cannot control. It is this dichotomy between ownership and control in the modern corporation that leaves so many social scientists uneasy with the Church's doctrine on private property as it now stands.

All of this is not to suggest that private property is no longer a meaningful reality. What it does suggest is that private property needs to be thoroughly re-analyzed in the light of the existing situation and that part of this re-analysis should include the question of the nature of large scale enterprises in a system wherein the government's function extends beyond providing police protection and welfare benefits into providing for the direction in which the economy should move.

As work must be done on the relation between the principles enunciated by the Council and economic planning and the modern corporation, so considerable work must also be done before the very positive principles for international economic cooperation will be converted into bases for concrete action. It is much too simple to interpret the statements of the Council Fathers as endorsements of foreign aid, Prebisch-like reform of trade, or United Nations policies for achieving a decade of development. But the Council Fathers do not endorse any such specific lines of action; instead they pass the obligation for defining the correct lines to where it belongs, namely, to "experts in such affairs" (CMW, 85).

What the Council, as Pope John before it, does do is to reject the international economic community as it now is structured. One might also safely argue that the Council likewise rejects a completely autonomous, self-regulating international economy

---

[12] CMW contains the interesting phraseology: "Private ownership or *some other kind of dominion* over material goods provides everyone with a wholly necessary area of independence . . ." Emphasis added.

of free trade and gold standard,[33] and in this regard is far more consistent than most economists who gladly argue for governmental action to ballance the national economy but for *laissez faire* to balance the international economy. International commodity stabilization proposals, differential trade preferences, international anti-trust laws, and even an international central bank all appear to be consistent with the Council's proposals. But none of them are necessarily consistent until "the experts" can reasonably show that world welfare is increased by such action.

In all three of the above areas, and there are others that could be noted, one can reconcile the general principles of the Council Fathers with specific lines of action. But to continue to do this solely on the level of generalization that is appropriate to a conciliar document is to play a game with reality that violates the scientific principles of economics that the Council so wholeheartedly recognizes.

V

What do the socioeconomic pronouncements of Vatican II mean to the modern world? To this observer, they mean three things. First, they mean that the leaders of the Roman Catholic Church are attempting to meet the world as it is, not as they might wish it to be. They have come forth with a resounding acceptance of Pope John's interpretation of this as being a world in the midst of ferment and change and yet with the potentiality of bringing mankind closer to the objectives of his creation than any previous structure he has lived within. They also accept it as a world that is moved primarily by men and not by history or harmony. And by accepting the world as being of this type, the Council Fathers are willing to give to men the right to direct the sectors of the world so as to bring into existence an optimum structure.

---

[13] Inasmuch as the Church rejects self-regulation of a national economy, it seems reasonable to assume that there is no valid reason for believing that self-regulation of the international economy is any more valid.

In the economic sphere Vatican II accepts the propositions that it is better to have economic growth than economic stagnation, economic stability than economic instability, and equitable economic distribution than inequitable economic distribution. It also recognizes, in this second meaning I see in the Council documents, that economic growth, stability, and distribution when correctly achieved mean increased human freedom on all levels. In this area Vatican II is in one sense an ecclesiastical endorsement of the main ends of economic life. But, as is the case with such endeavors as education, the Council emphasizes — as most Western economists also emphasize — that economic ends are subordinate to higher ends and that economic activities, therefore, are beneficial only to the extent that they do not violate such higher ends. What is of most importance, however, is not that the Council sees economic objectives as subordinate to other considerations but that it sees economic objectives as necessary for the achievement of these other considerations.

Finally, I am convinced, and I believe that the churchmen who composed Vatican II are also, that the socioeconomic pronouncements of the Second Vatican Council are only as meaningful as nonchurchmen will make them in the time to come. The program proclaimed by Pope Paul on December 7, 1965, is, as its instigators know, "but a general one" that "will have to be followed up and amplified" (CMW, 91). Unless appropriately trained people, and this especially involves laymen, turn to the detailed and difficult task of taking a close and a scientific look at "the signs of the times" and of applying the general notations of Vatican II to what these signs really are, all of the emphasis of the Council Fathers on justice, equity, and humanity will become noble statements surrounding a hollow core of nothingness.

This "new stage of history" is, as the Council Fathers know, one that has been created "by the intelligence and creative energies of man" channeled in what is normally called a scientific approach (CMW, 4). When dealing with concrete issues of socioeconomic life, this approach demands facts, theories, and detailed analysis. Only when man is in possession of these will it be possible to apply efficiently the general principles set forth at Vatican II. Thus the true evaluation of the meaning of the socioeconomic pronouncements of the Second Vatican Council will come out of the work or nonwork of "experts" in the socioeconomic fields.

CHAPTER VIII

THE CONSTITUTION ON THE CHURCH IN THE MODERN WORLD AND POLITICAL DEVELOPMENT

Dr. Victor C. Ferkiss

At the outset I must admit that it is with much trepidation that I write on this subject, and affirming this is not merely a conventional formality. I am not a specialist in theology or ethics, nor have I been as close a student of the development of the social doctrine of the Church as some of my colleagues. I have not attended the deliberations of the Vatican Council, much less participated in them. I can only react to this document in terms of my existential position — as a social scientist, a citizen, and one who considers himself a Christian.

These marginal qualifications to treat of my subject bear especially heavily upon me in that much of what I have to say may seem to many hypercritical. I cannot help feeling about this document and indeed about much of the work of the Council that, while a great event has occurred in the Church in the process of renewal, it has not gone far enough. We have moved in a few years over the intellectual terrain of centuries, but I fear that what we have done is jump from the fourteenth century into the nineteenth, a stupendous achievement, but yet not enough. I cannot help detecting a kind of gigantic failure of nerve, exemplified by what seems to me a tendency now to embrace as Christian all the clichés of the modernity of the day before yesterday. If my judgments are harsh, false, or even simply incompetent, all I can plead in defense is that the *Constitution on the Church in the Modern World* is not merely or even primarily a juridical document, but an exercise in communication. If I misperceive its significance, I can only plead that the failure to communicate is unlikely to be purely onesided.

What is at issue in any discussion of the significance of the chapter on the life of the political community — and let me note at this point that all my references are to the text as published by the National Catholic Welfare Conference; if it misleads me that itself would seem to indicate that the basic document too easily lends itself to mistranslation and misinterpretation — what is at issue is one of the central problems of political philosophy, the relationship between ethical principles and political institutions. We can, I think, at the outset reject the equally untenable and mischievous propositions that there are no basic universal principles of social ethics or that if there are, they cannot be used as a standard to judge social reality, and confine ourselves to the real problems: viz., if ethics provides basic norms for judging institutions and actions, how particular and specific can these norms be and, once they have been agreed upon, how can they be implemented?

The *Constitution* sets forth a number of specific norms regarding institutions and their behavior, derived from more general ethical norms. Some of these specific norms, it appears to me, are highly novel and challengeable, others are highly specific perhaps to an undesirable degree.

At the outset let me note that, in its first paragraph, this chapter reiterates as a standard of judgment the hallowed concept of the "common good" (par. 73), a concept which can for most practical purposes be equated with the more homely one of the "public interest." This concept is under fire from many quarters today, from social scientists who argue — and this is of course essentially nothing new — that there is no such thing as the "public interest," and social life is nothing but the clash of self-seeking private wills, and a more diverse group who exalt the private worlds and destinies of individuals at the expense of common concerns. It is with great interest as well as some concern that I see that Father John Courtney Murray seems to lend support to this latter position by suggesting that the "human person" rather than the "common good" should be the touchstone of our ethical reckonings. He is, of course, quite right in noting that the alleged needs of the common good have often been used as a screen for oppression by tyrannical rulers, but there is no norm in the lexicon of social ethics of which this cannot be said. Personally, I am not yet ready to abandon completely the order of priorities implicit in the injunction to ask not what your country can do for you but what you can do for your country.

Taken as a whole, Paragraph 73 of the *Constitution* sets the stage for later discussion by taking note, approvingly, of the greater human desire "to play a greater part in organizing the life of the political community." One must note in passing that this coy rhetorical style — describing events or opinions with judgments of them embedded often in the tone of the description — is not uncommon in Vatican documents, and possesses great and often realized potentialities for confusing both the faithful and the general public. What is approved here is somewhat vague, since what seems to be involved is democracy defined as participation in politics by the masses of the people. This is a popular definition today throughout the world — even among scholars who should know better. But while, by its standards, one can distinguish between the inert masses of archaic authoritarian regimes in backward areas and the populations of more advanced nations, one cannot distinguish between the sham elections and demonstrations of one-party states, which not only allow but insist on their subjects' activity in politics and those relatively few nations where the citizenry has some hope of controlling the actions of their governments through regular political means. That part of the paragraph which is negative in intent is more direct, but the hampering of freedom, the victimization of the innocent, and the enthronement of selfish interests against which it declaims are recognized verbally at least as evils even by the very regimes which practice these policies.

Paragraph 74 is a good example of how the document tends to introduce fundamental issues without resolving them. At the outset, when it says "For this purpose they set up a political community which takes various forms," it talks the language of the theorists of the social contract. The irony is that when this was a popular doctrine the main body of Catholic opinion vigorously opposed it. Now when it is no longer taken as seriously as an explanation of the origins of the state as such — obviously particular constitutions are written frequently — it seems to be embraced, even though it is acknowledged that the political community is founded on human nature and God's creation and only the form it takes is a matter of the will of the citizenry.

This political order, it is stated, must operate within moral limits and aim at the common good. To the extant problems of defining the common good is added those posed by speaking of "a dynamic concept of that good." What this bow to fashionable, modern rhetoric accomplishes in clarifying social norms is of course unclear. This lack of practical specificity is underlined later in the paragraph:

> But where citizens are oppressed by a public authority overstepping its competence they should not protest against those things which are objectively required for the common good; but it is legitimate for them to defend their own rights and the rights of their fellow citizens against the abuse of this authority, while keeping within those limits drawn by the natural law and the Gospels.

What can this mean? Does it mean, as it implies, in speaking of competence that injustice is a matter of jurisdiction, that a government only acts unjustly when it acts *ultra vires,* and cannot be indicted for acting in a substantively wrong fashion within its proper zone of responsibility? Almost certainly not.

But why the confusion? More seriously, does this passage mean to deny the right of revolution to Christians? This is the implication of speaking about obeying the proper laws of government and simply defending one's rights against implicitly specific abuses of authority. Of what guidance is all this to men like the late Father Torres and his fellow guerrilla priests in Latin America or for that matter to oppressed populations anywhere?

In the following paragraph, Paragraph 75, the *Constitution* says that, "It is in full conformity with human nature" that citizens should have various political rights, including "taking part . . . in the election of political leaders." Here again the coyness of ecclesiastical rhetoric confuses at least one simpleminded reader. Does this passage mean that free elections are permitted, that they are necessary to conform with human nature, or that they are an ideal? If the former, we have simply advanced beyond the clerical defenders of the *ancien régime;* if the latter, we have entered upon a concept which is slightly debatable but highly irrelevant. But if it is contended that all regimes not based on pure parliamentary democracy, in nineteenth-century, liberal style, are contrary to human nature, then it is being said that most of the regimes which now exist in the world are unnatural, virtually all which have ever existed were unnatural, and, if some of the more pessimistic conclusions which many of my colleagues draw from the political behavior of the emergent nations are correct, most of the world's political regimes in the foreseeable future will not be in conformity with human nature. Does the *Constitution* really intend to say this, with all its revolutionary implications both intellectually and practically, or is this another bow toward intellectual fashion?

The next passage says that there must be a "statute of positive law" providing for the structuring of political authority and the protection of human rights if the citizens' activity is to produce the good which is to be expected in the "normal" course of political life. A naïve interpretation would conclude that this means that written constitutions are necessary to normal human politics, so that even Great Britain is in danger of being considered an unnatural polity. More subtle exegetes tell me the passage does not really mean that, that "statute of positive law" is a clumsy translation. But what does it mean, then? And of what use are concepts — not about metaphysical nuances but about everyday political exigencies — which so easily lend themselves to mistranslation and misinterpretation?

Following this, still within Paragraph 75, there is a discussion of the role of the government in society. It begins with a re-affirmation of the traditional principle of subsidiarity, which as it always has rejects the alternatives of totalitarian control on the one hand, and absolute individualism on the other, without telling us where the proper boundaries of state action can be drawn within the vast range of possibilities between them. When later on the *Constitution* uses the word translated as "intervene" to speak of state action in social, economic, and cultural matters, it seems to beg the question of boundaries and ignore the salient fact that modern society constitutes a virtually seamless web of public and private activity. It also begs the question in speaking of the temporary restriction of the "exercise of rights" for the sake of the common good, which assumes the abnormality of government intervention in the unspecified contexts under consideration. Despite this, however, the passage in question allows sufficient freedom of maneuver to accommodate a Lyndon Johnson and a Barry Goldwater, and their more "extremist" partisans as well. The passage that tells us that citizens must be "patriotic" but not "narrow-minded" is in the same spirit. All of this would sound well in a political platform. Yet the Church is surely not running for office. Renewal cannot be purchased at the price of vagueness, triviality, and irrelevancy. Of these the unsaved world already has more than its share.

Before closing on a note of exhortation to the ennobling or political life, Paragraph 75 does make a minor breakthrough in recognizing that freedom of opinion must extend to groups as well as individuals if it is to be a meaningful reflection of human dignity. This is somewhat vitiated by the statement immediately following which says that political parties must pro-

mote those things which are required by the common good
rather than give their own interests priority. The role of political
parties in articulating and integrating particular interests within
society is simply more complex than this statement implies; indeed they may best fulfill their duty to the common good by being special pleaders for their members' and adherents' interests
just as a lawyer may serve justice by being effective as a onesided advocate of a particular cause. Wherever the truth lies,
there are depths to the problems discussed which it seems obvious are unknown to the framers of the *Constitution*.

We come finally to the Church and the state, or more properly
and realistically, the role of the Church in society. Here we are
on surer ground, perhaps more familiar ground to the framers
of the chapter under discussion.

The ideals are stated, but the obstacles to the ideals of
political freedom are nowhere discussed. We are all familiar
with what they are — overt ideological rejection of these ideals
on the part of totalitarian regimes, poverty, illiteracy, lack of a
sense of nationhood among many peoples and, it must be said,
the results of original sin, made evident in fundamental conflicts of interests among men which simply cannot be resolved
by democratic procedures. Some of these obstacles are discussed
elsewhere in the *Constitution* in their own terms, but such discussion is of little use unless it is related to its political ramifica-
tions. And what about the measures necessary to overcome these
obstacles: increased economic and political resources where
needed, political power sufficient to overcome ideological opposition by the totalitarians, great amounts of time in the case of
certain problems, and, let us say it, sheer physical coercive power
in some instances.

To realize the high ideals set forth in the *Constitution* means
that Christians must get down into the real world and dirty
their hands. Many despair of the possibility of doing this and
remaining Christian. Goethe said that the man of action is always
ruthless; no one has a conscience save the observer. He is wrong
of course, but the *Constitution* insofar as it applies to politics is

a document of conscience of little use to the man of action. It is an essentially utopian document, not in the sense that its desiderata are impossible of achievement, but that — partially because of their generality — we are given no guidance as to how to reach them.

Perhaps in the long run, however, this is all to the good. We have a statement of general aims. It is the task of the Christian, acting as a free and responsible human being, to provide the specifics and take the actions needed to create an order compatible — as far as man's fallen nature will allow — with the aims set forth. The *Constitution* is not a blueprint nor a set of marching orders, but a commission to act freely on the behalf of the Church and God. One cannot help wondering, however, whether the institutional Church realizes this and how it will react to such action.

CHAPTER IX

SOME COMMENTS ON CHAPTER V OF THE PASTORAL CONSTITUTION OF VATICAN COUNCIL II

Dr. Arnold S. Kaufman

My aim is to state the central argument of Chapter V of the *Pastoral Constitution* and to examine its soundness.

The basic conclusion is that peace requires mutual trust among nations. Peace is understood not simply as an absence of war, but more affirmatively as "an enterprise of justice." Indeed, the mutual trust mentioned in the chapter cannot be achieved unless nations are, in some sense, governed by sentiments of justice and love (or, as I prefer, benevolence. I regard "love" as too indiscriminate a term to use in this connection). It is also assumed that nations are today profoundly defective in these respects. There must, therefore, be a "change of heart." Given this change of heart, the creation of a universal public authority will become possible; for the establishment, authority, and efficacy of such a public order depends upon mutual trust. It is not clear to me whether the authors of the chapter also think of mutual trust as *enough* to insure the establishment of such a public authority

There are essentially two rational bases for trusting another person to behave in ways thought to be appropriate. Either his personal interests as he perceives them will be served, or he possesses certain moral attitudes that provide a motive for the expected action. The first is based on calculations about someone's perceived self-interest; and I term it "calculated trust." The second is based on the belief that one has a conscientious desire to fulfill obligations for no reason other than that the agent regards it as morally right to do so. I term this second sort of trust, "conscientious trust." Of course, these motives may be mixed in any concrete situation.

One person's caculated trust in another may be reasonable either because the latter believes that he has a productive interest in acting in the specified way, or because he is convinced that compliance alone will enable him to avoid threats to his well-being. A businessman may be trusted to observe an agreement if he thinks that there is profit to be made by doing so. Similarly, he may also be trusted if he thinks non-compliance will result in penalty.

Vatican Council II affirms that *conscientious* trust is the indispensable condition of peace; for the mutual trust which it projects is rooted in traits of justice and benevolence. The Council is not so clear about the place it accords calculated trust. It does, however, recognize that threat of deterrence may play a vital role in the achievement of peace. It also sketches the long-term, productive interest that any state has in that achievement. At the same time it explicitly rejects the notion that peace can result from a balancing of powers alone. That is, it denies that it is possible to forge a system of trust based on mutual calculations of benefit and loss sufficient to insure peace. Thus, the Council rejects the purported wisdom of foreign policy realists like Thomas Hobbes, Hans Morgenthau, and Reinhold Niebuhr.

In this conflict between the views expressed by the Council and those held by foreign policy realists, my sympathies lie with the Council. But there are ways in which its arguments can be strengthened, and there are flaws that deserve criticism. Only a few of these points can be covered in this brief essay.

The first difficulty has to do with the fact that it is not the relations among individuals that are under discussion, but the relations among states. Though the difference is important, it is not sufficiently stressed by the Council. One can be reasonably sure that moral traits, once established, are fairly permanent properties of individuals; this is by no means obvious in the case of states. For one thing, those who have operative control of foreign policy change from time to time. For another, as Reinhold Niebuhr has stressed, though conscientious trust may be reasonable within small and intimate groups, it becomes less rational to suppose that men will act in the spirit of justice and benevolence in proportion to the size of the relevant collectivities. For the tendency to neglect the interests of those outside the group increases in proportion to the size of the group that acts. States are very large collectivities; the prospects for conscientious moral behavior are proportionately low.

Those who disagree with the realists can answer these arguments along two lines. First, it is after all individuals who act. If the individuals have the moral traits required, then their actions can reasonably be expected to be controlled by that fact to some extent at least. But, more important, the moral attitudes that men possess are powerfully shaped by the social environment of which they are a part. The cumulative impact of political, legal, educational, familial, and not least, religious institutions is enormous. To the extent that these institutional structures operate so as to build into people the appropriate moral attitudes, the probability that the agents who act for the state will express them in policy is increased. For example, it seems clear that President Kennedy's remarkable restraint after the disastrous Bay of Pigs landings as well as his agonizingly measured response during the Cuban missile crisis were both, in large part, due to the fact that he and certain important advisors were to some extent acting under moral — not just "political" — restraint.

As I see it, one of the basic problems that exists in the United States is the enormous gap that exists between the moral rhetoric and practice of most Americans. Or, to put it another way, the morality expressed verbally by most Americans is belied by their actual behavior. Nowhere is this more evident than in the making of foreign policy. The realists would claim that no special explanation is required. According to most realists, men are not merely "wounded by sin" — sin is indelibly etched in their souls. Given this basic nature of men, the gap between rhetoric and practice is inevitable. But for anyone who wishes to defend the possibility of conscientious trust among nations this explanation will not do. Instead, we must seek to determine just what it is about our institutions that produces the gap, and how, if desirable, it should be closed. For in an imperfect democracy like our own, the state will act in accord with justice and benevolence only if these traits are securely etched in the character of overwhelmingly large numbers of our citizens. Unless we know the institutional structures that inhibit the "change of heart" of which the Council speaks, and have a program for changing those institutions, then peace cannot be secured. The same is true for any other state — though institutional problems will differ depending on different structures of decision-making power.

It is at this point that I must express strong reservations about the Council document. It seems to envision the needed changes of heart as individual acts of moral regeneration relatively unconnected with any institutional structures other than those of organized religion: and, in particular, religious authority. As the document puts it:

> since the human will is unsteady and wounded by sin, the achievement of peace requires a constant mastering of passions and the vigilance of lawful authority.

(Given the tradition of natural law on which the entire argument is premised, I understand "lawful authority" to refer to those who are wise in moral matters, not public officials possessing a status of authority in public law.) Perhaps I read too much, or too little, into this passage. If so, I hope I shall be corrected.

In any event, my point is that however important may be the factors of individual willingness to submit to lawful authority or the capacity for moral regeneration, these factors are less significant than the total institutional milieu that exists. In other words, strongly rooted traits of justice and benevolence are *primarily* (not exclusively) the result of the quality of political, legal, economic, educational, industrial, and familial institutions that exist. For example, without industrial institutions that genuinely promote respect for the individual without a democratic process that genuinely promotes respect for each individual's power to seek and to know the truth independently of authority, and so on, the changes of heart called for by the Council cannot occur. In short, the changes of heart must be the outcome of political programs designed to produce institutional change — programs of the sort that are not permitted to exist say in Spain or either of the Vietnams, or either of the Chinas; that at present are permitted to exist only partially in nations like the United States and France. It is understandable why the Council did not recognize this truth explicitly, and advance an appropriate program. It is nevertheless one of the document's limitations.

Let me recapitulate the discussion to this point. With the Council's basic claim that calculated trust and the balance of power theory which it presupposes are not sufficient conditions of peace, I most emphatically agree. I agree also that conscientious trust among nations is possible and indispensable. But it is necessary to recognize that achievement of such trust between nations is a very different, more complex matter, than between individuals. That a change of heart in the sense of a general extension, deepening, and consolidation of the attitudes of justice and benevolence is necessary, is a premise which I also endorse. But the Council seems to suppose that this change of heart can come about primarily through efforts of moral regeneration induced by moral exhortation, and by respect for authority. This I very much doubt. What is needed in all societies of this world are the right sorts of institutional milieus, the forging of which requires sustained political action.

And now I move to a further point — the extent of the change required varies very much from society to society. There are even those who believe that for some societies the necessary reconstruction of social institutions requires bloody revolution. The Council's failure to discuss the problem of social revolution in anything like the detail required is another major omission. The Council alludes to this problem at only one point. It allows that "in many cases there is an urgent need to revamp economic and social structures." But then it continues, "But one must guard against proposed technical solutions that are untimely. This is particularly true of those solutions providing man with material conveniences, which are nevertheless contrary to man's spiritual nature and advancement" (94). This cryptic passage is not elaborated. Pope John in his *Pacem in Terris* gave point to this caution in the following passage:

> It must be born in mind that to proceed gradually is the law of life in all its expressions; therefore in human institutions, too, it is not possible to renovate for the better except by working from within them, gradually (par. 39).

Am I being hasty in supposing that in practice bloody revolution would in general be regarded by the members of the Council as the sort of untimely technical solution which they oppose?

In any event, the problem of maintaining world peace is intimately tied up with the problem of coping with revolutionary disorder in the world. To the extent that revolutionary movements are not involved as third parties, the Cold War among industrialized nations has grown increasingly cooler. The chief threat to the peace of the world has resulted from outside efforts to induce or to halt revolutionary action in the so-called "Third World." Vietnam, the Dominican Republic, Cuba, are the main instances in the recent past; the Lebanese and Suez crises in the more remote past. On the other side, Hungary and, to a lesser extent, Poland and East Germany are cases in point. And Peking's desire to foment revolutions is well-known.

Let us view this problem from the point of view of those

hostile to revolution. Put in its baldest terms, the pattern that has been established and which is now operative in Vietnam is the following: A revolutionary movement with some admixture of Communist elements moves to take power. The extent of the Communist penetration varies from case to case. (Read "capitalist" or "bourgeois" to get the picture from the point of view of the great Communist powers.) Some of the great Western powers see the development as a threat to the precarious balance of power that has been secured. They fear that to permit the revolutionary movement to triumph will whet the appetite of the adversary power, threaten the balance even more severely. Hence, they feel that a military response sufficient to avert the threat to balance of power is required. In the final analysis, this is the rationale of America's Vietnamese policy — all talk about our commitments, and concern for the preservation of free, self-governing communities notwithstanding. But military intervention by one great power frequently brings the threat of military intervention by another. There is steady escalation until and unless the great power comes to its senses (as we did at the time of the Bay of Pigs) or until some other great power tips the balance decisively against further escalation (as we did at the time of Suez and the Russians did in Laos).

If the gravest threat to peace now for the forseeable future comes, as I think, from the enlargement of conflicts that start originally as local revolutionary action, then the Council's neglect of the problem of social revolution is a very important gap in its proposals. If Pope John's statement in his, in many ways, magnificent encyclical letter can reasonably be taken as the official Catholic position — a supplement to the Council's views — then the defect is more substantial. For my own view is that the gravest threat to peace today comes from those whose reactions to revolutionary disorder are controlled neither by the spirit of justice nor benevolence, but are, in the crudest terms, expressions of a self-righteous desire to preserve the prevailing balance of power. And I say this without for a moment denying that those who promote revolutionary disorder as a means of promoting national aspirations also threaten the peace. But the latter threaten peace less because they miscalculate the extent to which successful revolutionary movements can be converted into instruments of national policy. Russia's mistake in Yugoslavia is being duplicated by China in many areas of Asia and Africa.

Too many of the men who make foreign policy in the more developed nations of the world view the ferment in under-developed countries from the lofty height of a judging deity. Their implacable lack of compassion effectively screens out the agony that is the daily lot of millions of individual human beings in the poorer nations of the world. Analyzing Dean Rusk's contributions during the life of the Kennedy administration, Arthur Schlesinger, Jr. had this to say:

> At times one wondered whether the harshness of life — the seething planet of revolutionary violence, ferocity and hate, shadowed by nuclear holocaust — ever penetrated the screen of cliches, ever shook that imperturbable blandness.[1]

The moral insensitivity portrayed is not, however, a merely personal fault. Rather, to apply a point made earlier, it is a chronic disorder resulting from an institutional milieu that encourages us to view human beings as mere things, instruments of policy in the gigantic clash between the forces of light and the forces of darkness. Beneath the "imperturbable blandness" of men like Rusk is a controlling passion for abstract freedom, abstract democracy, and even for peace that is as ferocious in its consequences as the commitment of the inquisitors. Here indeed there is need for a national change of heart — one that is not likely to come about without a change of personnel.

Of compassion there is no lack in either the Council's statement or in Pope John's encyclical letter. Quite the reverse. Both, and especially the latter, are pervaded by a sense of compassion sufficient to make the most insensitive realist in

---

[1] Arthur Schlesinger, Jr., *A Thousand Days* (New York: Harper, 1964), p. 434.

foreign policy grind his teeth in despair. But compassion is not policy. And I cannot agree that Pope John's blanket condemnation of revolutionary action is the basis of good policy. The sweeping generalization that gradualism is always best is supported neither by the record of history nor by the facts of misery, power, and greed in the world today. The American Revolution is a case in point. The Mexican Revolution would appear to be another. As a CBS Report put it, the relative stability of Mexico is not unconnected with the fact that the revolutionary forces won out and thereupon set in motion a dynamic of reform and development. Again, who is to say that the prospects for the Black South Africans are better in the absence of revolutionary disorder? Is it possible to believe that the institutionalized greed and tyranny of the present South African regime can be made to give way without bloody revolution? And what about the Hungarian Revolution? I appeal to less controversial cases partly to rebut Pope John's sweeping generalization, partly because this is not the place to go into detail about more problematic revolutions such as those that have taken place in Cuba, the Dominican Republic, Algeria, and so on.

The former United Nations representative to Katanga, Conor Cruise O'Brien, recently wrote about the problem of bloody revolution in the "Third World" in the following acutely analytical terms:

> In the poor world, . . . the oppressed are not minorities but the masses, and they are confronted by ruling classes that cling avidly to their traditional large share of scarce resources. The interests of the ruling classes are simply not consistent with any social change in the interests of the people as a whole. The landowners, userers, sweat-shop owners, corrupt political bosses, and parasitic bureaucrats who now control in varying combinations most governments of the third world are precisely those people who must be deprived of their *raison d'être* if there is to be a social revolution. Why should these people allow themselves to be peacefully ousted as long as they have the money to pay others to de-

fend their interests? Such defense need not always be as obvious as the employment of white mercenaries by the government of the Congo. Rulers of most poor countries, by reason of that very poverty, can recruit mercenaries from among their own people. This method is less conspicuous than the Congolese method, but it is also less reliable because the danger of defection and mutiny is inescapable when national forces are used in a revolutionary situation. This danger, in turn, can give rise to a demand for extra-national, counter-revolutionary forces — Belgian regular troops in the nominally independent Congo, French regular troops in nominally independent Gabon, U.S. regular troops in nominally independent Santo Domingo and South Vietnam. If this line of reasoning is correct, and recent history seems to support it, then it is not likely that social revolution will occur without political revolution; political revolution will be opposed by force, and cannot prevail without greater force.[2]

In the parts of the world that O'Brien has principally in mind, those genuinely concerned about the peace of the world should start with the presumption that revolution is justified — or so I believe. If the burden of proof falls on the revolutionaries in more developed countries, it surely falls on the gradualists in the poorest societies. Even if Pope John's generalization were sound, it would still not follow that revolutionary movements ought to be opposed by great powers. That is, even if revolutions are never justified, it would not follow that interference by great powers is justified. In general, revolutions are the product of human misery sufficiently intense for men to put their lives and the lives of those they love in jeopardy. To intervene militarily in order to preserve the balance of power is often to compound the mischief that the revolution may itself be doing. For many of those opposed to American policy in Vietnam — those who have no illusions about the quality of the regime that would result were the National Liberation Front to come to power in South Vietnam, those who are *against* American policy and *not for* either the Viet

---

[2] Conor Cruise O'Brien, *The Counterrevolutionary Reflex* (The Columbia University Forum, Spring, 1966), p. 21.

Cong or China — it is indeed the belief that American military intervention has compounded the misery of the Vietnamese people, has diminished rather than increased the prospects of that unhappy land, that forms an important part of the basis for their opposition.

Revolution may then be the best way to win rights, to restore human dignity, to create the institutional milieu in which the sentiments of justice and benevolence may flourish. But even if this were not so, it might still be desirable to support bloody revolution, or at least not to oppose it, once it has, for whatever reasons, begun. For the alternatives at that point are not evolution or revolution, but rather successful, if bloody, revolution or bloody suppression. And it surely cannot be obvious that bloodshed in putting down revolt is always better than the shedding of blood involved in making a revolution.

I have devoted my remarks to criticism of Chapter V. But I would be remiss were I not to indicate how congenial I find the general temper and thrust of the *Pastoral Constitution.* The insistence that morality is relevant to the making of foreign policy, that the belief in human dignity is the touchstone of all sound policy, that conscientious trust among nations is an indispensable condition of peace, that the arms race is an "utterly treacherous trap," that a universal public authority must be forged — these are all views with which I heartily agree. It remains to translate these abstractions into sound political action — to convert the rhetoric into sustained pressure for a peaceful world. In doing so, it is not difficult to aid and abet the very forces that would empty the rhetoric of significant moral content, that would blunt the practical thrust. Personal ambition, convenience, ignorance, thoughtless subjection to authority — all contribute to such a blunting process. Those who, like the authors of the *Pastoral Constitution,* believe that the conduct of foreign policy should be principally controlled by moral considerations, should vigilantly guard against "bad faith" of this sort.

CHAPTER X

THE PASTORAL CONSTITUTION, WAR, AND DETERRENCE

Dr. William V. O'Brien

I propose to discuss the *Pastoral Constitution* from three angles. First, I will interpret the *Constitution's* handling of the major issues of war and peace confronting the world. Next, I will discuss the implications of the Council's statements on these issues for Catholics generally. Lastly, I will consider the implications of the *Constitution* for American Catholics, for the American hierarchy and its instrumentalities, and for American Catholic institutions of higher education and research.

THE COUNCIL ON THE GREAT ISSUES OF WAR AND PEACE

There have always been differences of opinion over the best way to "foster peace" or to foster discussions and actions that might foster peace. Some feel that the best way is to "think peace," "talk peace," "do peace." Others of a more pessimistic bent approach the subject first in terms of thinking about war and what can be done to prevent or mitigate it. This often involves thinking about wars designed to prevent or mitigate other wars. While contemporary papal and other authoritative Church teaching has continued to concern itself with the moral limits of just wars, it has generally tended to adopt the "positive" approach of thinking, talking, and doing peace.

This tendency has inevitably resulted in a tension between modern Catholic thought and the beliefs and actions of Catholics in the principal Western nations. For it is well-known that what modest peace we have is based on the threat to engage in wars so terrible as to deter major resort to armed force.

I would stress from the outset that this tension does not obtain simply between the teachings of the Church and some small elite of "hard liners" or "Cold Warriors." Nuclear deterrence is no secret. In every year since 1945, Catholics in countries which either possessed such deterrents or which were protected by them have acquiesced in the deterrent system and have elected to office officials whose foreign and defense policies were based in large measure on nuclear deterrence and other military preparations the morality of which is controversial. The point that I am making is that while some internationalists tend to snort at approaches to peace that begin with emphasis on management of war it is the near universal practice of nations to take exactly such an approach to their foreign affairs and defense problems.

The *Pastoral Constitution* is reasonably successful in acknowledging this tension between the "is" and the "ought" of international politics insofar as the nuclear problem is concerned. In my opinion, it is not satisfactory in its handling of the dynamics of international politics. But the treatment of the nuclear deterrence issues is sufficiently realistic to help us in the little time that is left us to come to grips with it. This is especially gratifying in view of the fact that the original draft of the Schema from which the *Constitution* developed was quite inadequate and incomplete in its treatment of this critical subject.

Essentially, the sections on war and peace begin with a repudiation of modern war as an instrument of foreign policy. In effect, the presumption is always against war as a moral and rational instrument of policy. However, once this is firmly established, it is acknowledged that the presumption against war can be overcome. This is the classic just war formulation which we find, for example, in St. Thomas' treatment which begins with the question whether it is ever not a sin to engage in war (see *Constitution*, Art. 77).

The presumption against war can and must be overcome in certain circumstances. This is so because of the perennial need for force in human society. The Council echoes the sentiments of all recent popes who, as was the case in Pope Paul's address to the UN, call for peace but recognize that as long as man is sinful and imperfect there will be a need for coercive sanctions to protect the innocent and society (Art. 78, par. 6).

So, while the Council appears to place a heavy burden of proof on those who initiate and support allegedly just wars, it clearly rejects pacifism as the official doctrine of the Church. Nevertheless, as we know, the Council reversed the doctrine as expounded by modern popes insofar as conscientious objection is concerned (Art. 78, par. 5). Some of us would hope that once the right of conscientious objection is conceded, its more vocal exponents would disengage themselves from debates over the nuances of military strategy; but that hope is not confidently entertained.

The *Constitution* apparently further reinforces its acknowledgement of the perennial need to protect the internal and external security of political societies by its praise of the military profession (Art. 79, par. 5).

Within this context of a strong general warning against the dangers of war and an acknowledgment of the occasional necessity and justice of recourse to war, let us examine the implications of the *Constitution's* treatment of modern war and deterrence.

It must be acknowledged that this treatment leaves many unanswered questions. The Council Fathers join the modern popes in condemning "total war" (Art. 80, par. 3). It is not entirely clear whether that means nuclear war or total war in the manner of World War II.

But let us set that issue aside and go directly to the heart of the matter. The Council clearly condemns counter-city warfare.

Any act of war aimed indiscriminately at the destruction

of entire cities or extensive areas along with their population is a crime against God and man himself. It merits unequivocal and unhesitating condemnation (Art. 80, par. 4).

This is in the context a very strong statement to the effect that acts contrary to the *universal natural law* are never permitted (Art. 79, par. 2). Had the Council left the subject at that, as the original draft Schema did in effect, it would by implication have condemned strategic nuclear deterrence. For it is well-known that such deterrence rests on a credible willingness to destroy an enemy's cities if he destroys yours. If such an act is immoral, it is presumably not rendered permissible because another party has committed it first to your detriment.

In this connection, one can only speculate over the implications of the Council's failure even to mention the principle of noncombatant immunity from direct, intentional attack. Among scholars and publicists who write about war in terms of traditional, natural law doctrines it is common to refer to this principle as a fundamental, perennial principle of natural law. Insistence on this point leads to a number of positions, among which the following may be distinguished:

　1) general or nuclear pacifism;

　2) modified just war positions based on interpretations of the principle which permit use of modern means of warfare, e.g., on the grounds that attacks against population centers are not made with the primary intention of killing noncombatants but of destroying military objectives, or on the grounds that most of the attacked population can fairly be said to be part of "the war effort" and consequently does not deserve the immunity of "noncombatants" (or "innocents").

　3) just war positions that do not accept the contention that the principle of noncombatant immunity as traditionally interpreted is a necessary, immutable principle of natural law but who hold, rather, that it was a rule of customary law arising out of the military practices of the late Middle Ages and hence neither wholly binding nor practically feasible in modern warfare.

The Council did not refer explicitly to this principle nor to the controversy over its validity and meaning. In its treatment of "total" war and nuclear war it seemed to have given implicit support to the principle of noncombatant immunity in its condemnation of counter-city warfare but then to have left the question uncertain by failing to condemn strategic nuclear deterrence.

For the *Constitution* goes beyond general condemnations of extreme forms of nuclear war. It explicitly confronts the central fact of the deterrence system which is the basis for the international system. This fact is neither condemned nor approved. Both its importance and its dangerous character are underscored and we are all urged to do everything that we can to conceive and execute an escape from this "treacherous trap" (Art. 81, par. 2).

Thus the Council did not draw the conclusion which would seem to flow from the judgment that

> Whatever be the facts about this method of deterrence, men should be convinced that the arms race in which an already considerable number of countries are engaged is not a safe way to preserve a steady peace, nor is the so-called balance resulting from this race a sure and authentic peace. Rather than being eliminated thereby, the causes of war are in danger of being gradually aggravated. While extravagant sums are being spent for the furnishing of ever new weapons, an adequate remedy cannot be provided for the multiple miseries afflicting the whole modern world. Disagreements between nations are not really and radically healed; on the contrary, they spread the infection to other parts of the earth. New approaches based on reformed attitudes must be taken to remove this trap and to emancipate the world from its crushing anxiety through the restoration of genuine peace (Art. 81, par. 2).

The Council, then, calls attention to the fact of deterrence and its dangers. It says that there are some who say that this can be an adequate basis for international order, then it leaves the subject. It raises a question and then leaves it. It does not condemn deterrence. It does not explicitly approve it and say, "Well, we have decided that it really is necessary although it is very unpleasant." It simply leaves the subject open, which then puts us in something of a dilemma because in Article 80, paragraph 4, indiscriminate warfare is branded as immoral, a sin. But the Council Fathers seem not to have been prepared to dot the "i" and cross the "t" and say, "And so, therefore, the kind of deterrent threats that are presently made by all the nuclear nations are threats to do something that is immoral." But the Council does not reach this conclusion explicitly.

This, then, leaves to those who one way or another support or benefit from strategic nuclear deterrence a little more time to find ways of avoiding reliance on such morally controversial preparations and plans. It may be that now or in the future various forms of counter-force or graduated deterrence of warfare will be sufficient to deter nuclear attack and it will not be necessary to contemplate the necessity of doing what the Council seems to condemn. It may be that progress in arms control and disarmament will produce an inching down from the present dangerous nuclear peace until deterrence on all sides is based on means that are not so objectionable. Or it may be that international conflicts and differences will abate to the point where it will be unnecessary to base the whole international system on threats and military preparations. Now, as to the last possibility, it is to be regretted that the Council did not address itself to the continuing problem of ideologically rooted conflict. In this respect it does not meet the standards set by *Pacem in Terris* wherein Pope John recognized the obstacles that such conflicts create insofar as peace and arms control and disarmament are concerned. This is too bad because serious pursuit of the goals of international law and order, arms control and disarmament must begin with the clear recognition that the world is seriously divided and that our goal is, as one international lawyer[1]

---

[1] Myres S. McDougal and Florentino P. Feliciano, *Law and Minimum World Public Order: The Legal Regulation of International Coercion* (New Haven/London: Yale University Press, 1961).

calls it, "minimum world public order" based on a very modest and precarious consensus on such subjects as the inadvisability of mutual annihilation, rather than an advanced world order based on a high incidence of shared values among the nations and blocs of the world.

GENERAL IMPLICATIONS OF THE
PASTORAL CONSTITUTION'S SECTIONS ON WAR AND PEACE

It seems to be well-established that the section of the *Constitution* dealing with war and peace is not designed primarily to give definitive doctrinal answers but to raise issues and to exhort us — perhaps command us — to work toward their solution. There is a note in the *Constitution* reminiscent of the "all deliberate speed" admonition in the *Brown* v. *Board of Education* case. The majority of the Council Fathers seem to have recognized that they were not ready to propose final solutions to the moral dilemmas of the nuclear age. The majority also seem to have acknowledged that it would not be prudent to demand a sudden, revolutionary change in the political-military policies and preparations of the West in a world of conflict, much of which emanates from states which could not be expected to heed the moral imperatives of the Catholic Church.

At the same time, it cannot be said too strongly that the Council Fathers are raising issues on which all of us are expected to act now. Whatever our competence and responsibility, we all have a moral obligation to contribute to the processes by which nations escape the treacherous trap.

THE CHALLENGE TO THE
CATHOLIC CHURCH IN THE UNITED STATES

The United States is the principal Western nuclear power. Its nuclear deterrent covers dozens of nations. Every hour of the day the United States is preparing to engage in the execution of its deterrent threat in a strategic nuclear war. Although such a war might not escape human control, it would certainly involve indiscriminate destruction. No American Catholic layman, priest, or bishop can avoid the moral responsibility for subjecting the policy of deterrence to moral analysis. Yet this is one of the least and most inadequately discussed subjects in the world of the contemporary American Catholic community. The *Pastoral Constitution* — only reinforcing common sense — enjoins us to subject this overarching fact of national and international life to moral analysis and to seek policies that are possible and morally justified which may ameliorate our present situation which is physically and morally dangerous.

So there should be study and discussion. Part of the discussion will take the form of feature articles in the Catholic press, letters to the editor, round-ups of doctrinal and personal condemnations and approvals, summary replies by the misunderstood and maligned authors of the feature articles, "To-be-continued-next-week" exchanges on the subject between friendly or not-so-friendly rivals amongst the Lippmans and Alsops of the Catholic Press, etc. All of this is a part and a necessary part of the process of awakening American Catholics to their responsibilities as citizens of the world's leading nuclear power. All manner of conferences, addresses, and the like are also in order.

But discussion of this kind must also be accompanied by serious research and technical discussions embracing both the empirical data and the moral principles at issue. How well is the Church in the United States prepared for such research and discussion?

We might find the answer by conducting a little quiz:

1) Name five American Catholic scholars who could be nominated for a commission to advise the Pope on the problems of morality, modern war, and deterrence. (They should be at least as qualified as the members of the committee advising the Pope on the population problem.)

2) Name three Catholic academic centers of research on this subject, state their principal contributions, and mention their publications which one might consult in order to learn more about these problems.

3) Name six American bishops who have a justified reputation for concern and competence on this subject.

4) Name one editor of a Catholic newspaper or journal of opinion who, having published vehement pacifist condemnations of all that the deterrent state of America stands for, advocated a renunciation as a citizen of all the policies and activities of said deterrent states in the manner so forthrightly suggested by Walter Stein.[2]

5) Name the officers of the USCC and/or offices that international affairs specialists of the National Council of Churches or any other Protestant or Jewish full-time specialists in such matters would contact to discuss the issues we have been discussing here. Of course we all know what the answer to that question has been for many years: Msgr. George Higgins' Social Action Department consisting of himself, Father John Cronin, and a tiny secretarial staff that regularly has performed miracles. This, by and large, was the office designated by the American Bishops to cover subject matter within the jurisdiction not only of the Departments of Labor, HEW, Commerce, Interior, Justice, and Treasury, but also of the Departments of State and Defense. The Church in the United States has been able to afford many things but until recently it could not find justification for budgetary support of a permanent, professional Department of International Affairs to advise the American Bishops on questions such as the morality of the nuclear deterrent on which all U. S. foreign and military policy is based.

[Since this symposium the Bishops have, in May, 1967, organized a U. S. Bishops' Committee for World Justice and Peace and have opened an office under the direction of Msgr. Marvin Bordelon in Washington. This development follows the lead of the Holy Father in establishing a pontifical commission on Justice and Peace in Rome. It is hoped that this will be the beginning of a systematic and strongly supported effort to create organizations and to recruit experts in all relevant

---

[2] Walter Stein (ed.), *Nuclear Weapons and Christian Conscience* (London: Merlin Press, 1961).

fields sufficient to the challenges that modern international problems present to the Catholic Church in America.]

The process of producing the *Pastoral Constitution on the Church in the Modern World* surely demonstrated to anyone who was interested that, having "lucked out" this time, the Church generally and the American Catholic Church in particular was faced with the urgent necessity of organizing itself in such a way as to permit the mobilization of all the relevant *expertise* of American Catholics when a great and complicated moral issue required study and discussion.

It is all very well for bishops in Holland or India to condemn nuclear war as immoral. For them it is not unlike people in Montana condemning racial injustice in Birmingham and Los Angeles. Such condemnations, in a sense, are not news. But American bishops and American Catholics are in the nuclear equivalent of Birmingham and Los Angeles. Let there be no underestimating their dilemma. They literally hold in their hands, and we with them, questions such as this:

1) Will the day come when an American Catholic cannot in conscience run for the office of President because, as Commander-in-Chief, he would have to direct preparations and perhaps actions which his Church has condemned as immoral? For that matter, has it come?

2) Will the day come when all practicing Catholics can be rightly classified as conscientious objectors? What is the true future of American Catholics in the professional ranks of the armed forces? Should a Catholic university invite the commander of the Strategic Air Command to address a commencement audience?

In asking these questions I am seeking to penetrate the fog of apathy that has surrounded this subject matter in this country. I am not for a minute suggesting that we should start with the idea that the United States has the moral right to take any measures that it deems necessary and that the object of an inquiry into the morality of war is to find justifications and excuses for everything that this country has done or might have to do. I am suggesting that the reconciliation of the right of strong condemnations by the Church of the principal means of defense is a difficult — perhaps impossible — task. Serious efforts to deal with this dilemma are long overdue. We can "foster" peace in many gratifying, positive ways. But unless we deal with this grim and unpleasant problem of war and deterrence no so-called positive measures are going to produce the peace that the *Pastoral Constitution* and all of us seek.

CHAPTER XI

ROLE OF THE LAYMAN

Dr. John J. Figueroa

I must make it clear that I am not offering a paper in the usual sense. I was originally asked to do this, and then I was asked if I could come for the whole week to listen to what was going on, take part, and then attempt, in the light of what had been said, to make some comment, suggest some topics for discussion on this question of the layman in the Church today.

The first thing I would like to say is that various things have worried me considerably, and I am saying these things that we may discuss them; I know that very few of us feel that we really have the answers.

It seems to me that there is a necessary sort of binary arrangement in our thinking about these matters. I heard somebody say the other day that we must get rid of transcendence. We must apparently stick with immanence. I frankly do not understand what this means. I do not understand what it means to be a Christian without reference to something other than the mess in which we find ourselves.

So it seems to me that maybe my language is too old-fashioned. If anyone has better, newer language which would replace it, let him state it. There are so many things to be balanced. You have to balance immanence and transcendence.

Likewise, I do not understand the plea that we get rid of religion. I do not understand this.

The whole situation in which the human being finds himself — it seems to me — is a sort of double situation, one which
calls for the "binary approach." You think of the Church; you
have lay and cleric; you have the inward-looking and the
outward-looking; you have the detached and the committed;
you have the local Church and the universal Church; you have
the faith of the people, and the organization of the people, etc.
And I am very much afraid that because all of us have seen
dreadful weaknesses in the overemphasis in any of these, because of impatience and, in the end, I suppose, a lack of faith,
or lack of a heroic faith, and because we feel great urgency,
our reaction is: "Well, X has been stressed. . . . To hell with it!
The whole world is Y." Or "Y has been stressed. . . . Let's
forget that." And so on. I do not know any philosophy, including existentialism, which does not have a sort of duality, which
cannot in fact be mistakenly looked at on one plane only. Is
not this fact rooted in the very existence of man: the moment
you say he is individual, you have to say he is social; the
moment you say he is social, you have to say he is individual.

You see, St. Paul has this to say: (Is it completely meaningless; or is it a bad translation; or is it that I just don't understand it?)

> It is by letting the spirit lead you that you free yourselves
> from the yoke of the law.

> It is easy to see what effects proceed from corrupt nature.
> They are such things as adultery, impurity, incontinence,
> luxury, idolatry, witchcraft, feuds, quarrels, jealousies, out-
> bursts of anger, rivalry, dissensions, factions, spite, murder,
> drunkenness, and debauchery. Whereas the spirit yields a
> harvest of love, joy, peace, patience, kindness, generosity,
> forbearance, gentleness, faith, courtesy, temperance, purity.

Now, where are we? Are we really saying that this idea of
something being corrupt in us or in the world is something we
have misunderstood? Is this no longer a part of Christianity?
If it is a part of Christianity, can the very *easy* solutions that
some of us have been putting forward really work? Or have we

got to take into account the fountainhead (St. Paul calls it "corrupt nature") of feuds, dissensions, adultery, and the rest?

You might remember also the story of Nehemiah. He got up (with Ezra) to read from the Law of Moses to the people; it was a feast day. And when he started to read, they started to weep. And he said to them:

> Go home, and regale yourselves with rich meat and honeyed wine, sharing your good things with those who have none. There must be no sadness on this day, the Lord's feast day. To rejoice in the Lord, there lies our strength.

But they wept. Because I think these two things are inextricably bound up: the Law and Love; feasting and recalling previous hard days; servitude and release from servitude. And I don't see the sense of saying in any serious way that one is a Christian if one really thinks that he can go "straight to heaven in an air conditioned pullman" as was said of a great French writer. You know, I am not sure that this one really works at all. But I have noticed a tendency to feel that being both a Christian and a member of the modern world are rather easy, really — if only one would do this or do that. . . .

Recall what Bishop Wright had to say:

> One suspects that Pope John called the Council to provide just such a providential planting of certain seed ideas against *the severe winter of unbelief,* of scientism, atheist humanism and moral scepticism, all of which lie between us and the next springtime for both Christian faith and human hopes.

Now I know that Bishop Wright was not full of the spirit of magisterial certainty, for he himself said "So much for infallibility." I am merely saying that here is a man who was in the midst of the thing, and whose interpretation of Pope John was not of one who thought that he was merely opening a window. . . . you know . . . the oxygen would come in and from then on everything would be *so* healthy and *so* happy. When we open the windows, as we must, we know that we let in other things than pure oxygen. After all, Father Murray has already noted that we have to face the probability that the Council documents, and that the Council considerations, might in fact lead to a loss of people to Christianity and to religion. This is a necessary outcome of unstressing fear and of pressing for "freedom."

The other thing that Bishop Wright insisted on — perhaps he even cruelly overdid it — was that we have to realize that the world is a little bit larger than, shall we say, the Iberian peninsula. Even if you throw France in, or the enormous and powerful country of the United States of America, there is still a lot left. Much went on before these places were functioning; much is going on now. The world, and indeed the Christian world, is larger than the Reformation and the Counter-reformation. And I was very glad that Bishop Wright attempted to shake us from the culture-bound view of the world and of Christianity.

For instance, we've had interesting arguments about two-party, one-party states, about whether revolution is right, and so on. In some places, other than the States, the question about revolution is not a question at all. In some places you cannot live — if you are not a revolutionary. All Christians are *not* living in the same sort of society; and this applies to all our human brothers.

So I would like to ask you to think about the binary oppositions I mentioned. Unfortunately, the terms *optimism* and *pessimism* were used; and I think I was put in the pessimist camp. They are not good terms. I think that if you are going to be seriously hopeful about the future — whatever the future might be — you cannot just take a light view about what Bishop Wright called *the winter of unbelief* — I suspect that my friends — and I say this in all charity — that my friends in this country, even those who have worked so dedicatedly in the missionary fields, have been somehow inexplicably cut off from what Bishop Wright was explaining. Certainly when I knew Paris and London in my graduate days it was already quite clear that God and religion, and all that, were utterly irrelevant and meaningless to the vast majority of even the best students,

completely and utterly. What Dr. Shuster said is my experience
all over the world: Africa, Great Britain, this country. If you
are at any important conference — whether political or educational — if you think of getting out to Mass on Sunday, you are
pretty certain that you are the only one *thinking* about it. Now,
merely going to Mass or going to church perhaps does not
matter. Maybe that is not true religion. But I do not think
people at such important conferences are thinking even about
what one might call true religion, either. And I think they
would think you very stupid, if you asked them, "Are you concerned with this at all?" It does not matter any more. It is completely gone. It is not related. And young people say this too.
Is not the winter of disbelief already with us?

Now, if this is the situation, then we must look at it, in order
to make sure that Christian hope will mean something. I am
not saying that you agree that this is the situation, but just
suppose that it is. And I am not saying that if it is I will retire
to the nearest bar and take the necessary precautions against
such a dreadful situation. But I think that there is no sense in
hiding; we must try to get at what *is* the situation; and because
some of us have grown up in circumstances where the only
people we know are people who are sound Catholics or Luther-
ans — sound, accepting, good religious people — we are just lacking in the experience of the modern world! You see, I had as a
tutor at London University — certainly one of the best tutors
I have ever had — a woman who was a member of the Communist Party, and never made any bones about this. We discussed
this business of unbelief all the time. I was in contact with this
nearly all the time, through her and also through people who
went to church merely as a social convention, from time to
time. I do not believe that this tutor and the other "atheists"
somehow or other just do not exist. I certainly cannot believe
that my tutor was not a good teacher; that she was not a good
woman. It is simply not possible. But I know she had to consider my concerns about religion misplaced if not ridiculous;
she could not understand them. When we drank in the pub, at

the end of a discussion, she would say: "John, I don't understand it. You speak such sense on most things, and then you try to get me interested in this thing. I mean, what is this concerned with? What's it all about?"

Well, I do not want to exaggerate. We are speaking of the modern world which encompasses a large area. Maybe real unbelief and the apparent irrelevancy of belief are not so strong in your country. And it is for you to judge this. When, however, we are speaking of the modern world, we are speaking of something a little bit larger even than some part of this country, which one of us might know very well. And I really would like you to consider what is exactly the meaning of that particular formulation "the winter of unbelief" — and is Bishop Wright correct that this winter of unbelief is here; and what is the layman's role in connection with this, and what the role of the whole church? We, perhaps, should concentrate on the layman's role.

So much for my more general remarks. I know that people have been very impatient in saying: "Oh, let's do something. Let's get a program out." My reply to this is that if you ask me to come with you to a certain parish that you know, or to a certain country, I can sit down with six of you, and we can all put our ideas together and try to do something. I don't think we can sit in this room and, in general, plan to do something for everybody. I think all of us must find tasks that need doing and work on them. And I am certain that we need the spirit of inquiry and the fruit of research. But I find it very difficult to be specific with people from all over this country, with all kinds of experiences, from South America, Africa, France, the West Indies, the United States. So the things that I'm going to suggest to the layman are related now to what I said about the apparent twofold situation, and the twofold nature of experience. My prejudice is that one of the special things that the layman has to consider is this business of *One World*.

If I may quote Teilhard, "Essential affinities, not ultimate hatred. The age of nations is passed. The task before us now,

if we would not perish, is to overcome our ancient prejudice and to build the earth." And notice that he has not said this
completely in the wide eyed way I might say it, because he says
"if we would not perish." So he is not merely saying only that
"building the earth" is the fruition of evolution. It would seem
to me that "building the earth" is one of the tasks the layman
really has to put his mind to. Notice that in other terms, in
economic terms, Dr. Murphy appeared to be saying something
like this.

We have again here a binary opposition. One of my difficulties
with Teilhard is that he seems to be saying that the development of the universe, of man, in a certain direction is inevitable.
But if it is inevitable, then we need not do anything about it.

This is an old problem. It was a problem with the Marxists.
This is one I always had with my tutor. Since you are in the
stream of history — and the stream of history is, according to
you, on your side, and is going to bring about all you feel should
happen, why bother me with it? That's the way the stream of
history operates.

If evolution *necessarily* finds its whatever-you-may-call-it in the
Omega point and the rest of it, then there is not much I can
do about it. What could our role be in a process that is inevitable
— though conscious? Obviously, I must be putting forward a very
simple-minded view! Is the binary nature of things not once
again evident here? In other words, as A. V. Judges says of
pragmatism and "the new education" in another context, "we
would do well to consider the acceptance of both a principle of
growth and a principle of stability; of action and reflection; of
works and faith; of the yogi and the commissar; of the *yin* and
the *yang;* of the practical instrumentalism of Martha and the
intuition of Mary.

"Martha, mind you, is a good girl. We must just make sure that
she does not overtax her resources."

Are we supposed to do something about self-consciousness?
We are conscious beings; does this remove all inevitability from
our world? It is not only in matters of evolution, but also in

questions of Christianity that this question arises. If God gives us grace, and so on, must we end up as we consciously think we should? What is the exact relationship between our awareness of the need for *One World* and the achievement of this Christian hope?

So that one thing with which the Christian layman, looking outward, must concern himself, is the building of the earth, the achievement of *One World*.

So much for an outward-looking matter. What of the something *inward*-looking? One urgently necessary for our consideration is to be found in the whole field that Father Thomas spoke about: that of sex, life, marriage. I am not one of the laymen who say that celibates should not speak about this field. That claim does not seem to me to make sense. But some of the things Father Thomas had to note sound very queer to me, as a man who has been married for many years and who has enjoyed sex for many years. Some of his comments sound very, very odd. Such as that a man always needs a woman's reassurance, especially with regard to his performance in the sexual act. And I suspect that they sound very odd because he is working as a scientist, as a celibate scientist, in a certain way. I suspect that. And I think that lay people in the Church, those who are married, have been very lax in not studying sex and love in marriage, and in not making a contribution to the Church by using their experience of what these, and of what marriage, mean. Only a married person can understand Churchill's story that the only time his marriage nearly broke up was when he decided, early in it, to take breakfast with his wife in the morning!

The kind of insight and knowledge needed in dealing with marriage and its successes and problems must be very difficult to get mainly from questionnaires and the confessional. And so you see here I'm speaking about confession, and never having heard one!

But I really feel that marriage is a field that the layman should study from a moral and theological point of view. And I pose the question here which I have not ever heard discussed. If the point that Father Thomas is putting – I am not saying it is his point – but it *is* often put, maintains that you ought to separate fairly clearly the business of the function of procreation from the function of what one might call fulfillment, expression, love, satisfaction, pleasure and all the rest, how do you draw the line in what is now called adultery? There is no danger of any children any longer, if you know what you're doing. You need self-fulfillment. You're in a difficult situation. You are in a far off country; the act is for fulfillment and satisfaction, *not* procreation, then why not have sexual intercourse with an equally-in-need-of-fulfillment partner? Are we willing to face the consequences of really working out the logical and psychological consequences of a separation of the aspect of procreation from the aspect of fulfillment? Or is it that we hear about (or know about) population problems, know about our own people having serious difficulties with family planning; and therefore are tempted to make a quick popular solution? I would like really to look into the implications of saying that you can legitimately separate the self-fulfillment from the procreation in any basic sense. This is a question mainly for laymen, with theological training, of course: laymen who, if they are honest, know all the rationalizations by which any healthy human being could justify the most "fulfilling" of human acts!

And may I say here that there is an ambiguity in the term *layman* which I would like to point to. Most of the contributors in this symposium were chosen because we are not laymen in what we have been asked to speak on. *Layman* might mean not clerical; *layman* in another use may mean *not too well-acquainted with the field*. I think it is important to keep in mind that even if you are a layman in the sense of being non-clerical, this does not give you a right to pronounce on subjects on which you have not got proper qualifications. Some of us are imitating some of the old-time priests, who just because they were priests felt that they could comment on anything, pronounce on anything. Some of us are beginning to feel that because we are lay-

men we can pronounce on anything, whether we have competence in the matter or not. Of course, many things we have
competence in, even in the Church! If we go to church every
Sunday because we feel we ought to, or because we have been
brought up to, and we are regularly subject to certain things,
such as bad sermons, then perhaps we have the competence to
speak, and to act, on such matters!

Some other things, now, continuing the inward, Church-
directed look. It seems to me that laymen could do something
more in connection with helping people in all kinds of universities. I do not mean only within their own fields. That is
obvious. We have heard here some non-clerics show how very
learned they are, what good scholars they are. But I would like
to mention one or two things about Newman Centers and so on.
I know a university which has about 6,000 Catholic students; it
has a total of about 25,000 students. There is one priest to serve
as chaplain to Catholic students. How can this one priest do it?
There are lots of laymen there who could help. Although they
have considered it their business to point out to the Bishop that
the arrangements are not suitable — which is also true — I doubt
that they have done anything to help. Yet it is clear that in education as in any other field we have to husband our resources.
Are we going to tread warily, individualistically, or are we going
to pool our efforts and resources? Must we not concentrate on
the university, and on the Catholics in the university? And on the
research which the university especially can provide?

Now this is not a matter of elites, or leaving anybody out
of it. If, for instance, we are looking after teacher training in a
new country, and we have to get 40,000 children all of a sudden
into schools, we do not try, first of all, to get the teachers for the
classes for 40,000. What we try to do is to train people who will
train the teachers to look after the children. Then we get "a
multiplier effect" going. It might well be that one of the things
we have to do is to help more and more laymen with solid training in theology, or whatever it might be, to do some of the jobs
which clerics now do in universities and elsewhere. But laymen

often give me the impression, not least of all in universities, of holding back, of being so concerned with their own teaching and publishing as not to bother to help the stumbling student, especially the student stumbling in matters of faith and general understanding.

Further, I agree with the point often made that laymen should have something to say about the kind of statues, chairs, buildings, etc. which form part of his parish. He should be consulted at the planning stage, not only at the time of paying.

Some people feel that if we do not change the hierarchy, we cannot do anything about all this. I am not sure — a little passive resistance is useful — even with the most highly placed people. Sometimes, I feel sure, the hierarchy would welcome a little push in certain directions, making their decisions easier!

Finally — the general point that worries me: to engage oneself with what *is* — is that to say "whatever is *is right*." When we speak of various cultures, we seem to remember that there are many ways of doing things. But when we speak of the "modern world," and the Church's ministry to it, are we saying that the way the industrial revolution developed in the United States of America is the only suitable, is in fact the best way for it to have developed? Now this calls for expertise to answer. And from the experts with us we have had somewhat different answers. Do we really have to take over all the values of our present world? Is this what Christianity is about?

Some people apparently feel the bandwagon is going very well, let's get on it! Do we not have an obligation to change as well as to accept the "modern world"? But are there not choices in the style of industrialization? Perhaps here again laymen might be closer to the living problem. Do we really want the whole world to be another "inner city"? Is this the Christian aim? Are the types of cities we have in the U. S. a necessary concomitant of entering the modern world? Maybe laymen, especially those in universities and business and the professions, should work on these problems — they often live closer to the tensions than do the clergy.

There were many other points raised. The following are worth recalling: (1) property — do we have to change our basic concept of what property is in a non-peasant world? (2) We are long on principles; short on methods. (3) We must work to reduce world tensions.

In the end, I think, we must ask ourselves whether we have given up all idea of transcendence. Have we come to the situation where we think that to be a good man, to be a good humanist, is quite enough because God made all of us, and Jesus, "Our Lord," was a charismatic leader who left a group of men to carry out some sort of large welfare operation — a group easily divided into lay and cleric, progressive and reactionary, good guys and bad guys?

Or do we call upon the God of Isaac, the God of Abraham, the God of Jacob? What — if the expression may be pardoned — in God's name do we mean when we say:

> Glory to God in the highest
> And on earth peace to men he loves
> We give you thanks for your great glory
> O Lord God, heavenly King
> God the Father Almighty . . .

and all the rest of it?

One of the remarkable experiences of the Georgetown Colloquium has been the celebration together and the offering together of the sacrifice of the Mass in a most decent, just, and proper fashion.

Is it not necessary for us all to relate that kind of celebration to our questions about immanence and transcendence, lay and cleric, the winter of disbelief, and the planting of that special winter wheat which will provide, in the spring we hope for, bread such as man has not tasted before?

BIBLIOGRAPHY

This list of books was originally prepared for the Georgetown University Colloquium on the Church in the Modern World. It owes its present form to the National Newman Apostolate which collated the original data and put the list together.

1. Vatican II Documents and Reports

Abbott, Walter M., S.J. (ed.). *The Documents of Vatican II.* New York: Guild Press, 1966.

Anderson, Floyd. (ed.). *Council Day Book.* Washington, D.C.: NCWC 1960.

Bea, Cardinal. *The Second Vatican Council.* Paulist Press, 1962.

Berard, Aram, S.J. (trans.). *Preparatory Reports: Second Vatican Council.* Philadelphia: Westminster Press.

Brown, Robert McAfee. *Observer in Rome.* New York: Doubleday, 1964.

Concilium. *Theology in the Age of Renewal.* Vol. VI. Glen Rock, N.J.: Paulist Press, 1965.

Congar, Yves, O.P. *Report from Rome On the Second Session of the Vatican Council.* London: Geoffrey Chapman, 1964.

Cunneen, Joseph E. *Looking Toward the Council.* New York: Herder & Herder, 1962.

Daniel-Rops, Henri. *The Second Vatican Council.* New York: Hawthorn, 1962.

Dupront, M.A. *Le Concile et les Conciles.* Paris: Edition due Cerf, 1960.

Falcone, Carls. *Pope John and the Council.* London: Weidenfeld and Nicholson, 1964.

Guitton, Jean. *Jean Guitton at the Council.* Chicago: Franciscan Herald Press, 1962.

Häring, Bernard. *The Johannine Council.* New York: Herder and Herder, 1963.

Houtart, Canon. *The Challenge to Change.* New York: Sheed and Ward, 1964.

Kaiser, Robert Blair. *Pope, Council and the World.* New York: Macmillan, 1963.

Küng, Hans. *The Council, Reform and Reunion.* New York: Sheed and Ward, 1962.

Lenski, Gerhard. *The Religious Factor.* New York: Doubleday, 1963.

MacEoin, Gary. *What Happened at Rome?* New York: Holt, Rinehart and Winston, 1966.

McMahon, Frances E. *A Catholic Looks at the World.* New York: Vanguard, 1945.

Montcheuil, Y. *Aspects of the Church.* Chicago: Fides, 1955.

Novak, Michael. *The Open Church.* London: Longman, 1964.

Rahner, Karl, S.J. et al (Forward by Bishop John J. Wright). *The Christian and the World.* New York: P. J. Kenedy, 1965.

Riga, Peter. *Catholic Thought in Crisis.* Milwaukee: Bruce, 1963.

Rynne, Xavier. *Letters from Vatican City.* New York: Doubleday: Image Paperback, 1964.

――― *The Second Session.* New York: Farrar, Straus, 1964.

――― *The Third Session. The Debates and Cecrees of Vatican Council II.* New York: Farrar, Straus and Giroux, 1965.

――― *The Fourth Session.* New York: Farrar, Straus, 1966.

Serafian, Michael. *The Pilgrim.* New York: Farrar, Straus, 1964.

Scharper, Philip, et al. *New Horizons in Catholic Thought.* New York: Sheed and Ward, 1964.

Tavard, George. *The Church Tomorrow.* New York: Herder and Herder, 1965.

Thils, Gustav. *Christian Attitudes.* Chicago: Scepter Press, 1959.

Van Leeuven, Arend. *Christianity in World History.* Edinburgh House, 1964.

2. The Church in the Modern World

Cox, Harvey. *The Secular City.* New York: Macmillan, 1965.

Cross, Robert D. *The Emergence of Liberal Catholicism in America.* Cambridge: Harvard University Press, 1958.

Danielou, J. *The Lord of History.* Chicago: Regnery, 1958.

D'Arcy, M.C. *The Meaning and Matter of History.* New York: Farrar, Straus and Cudahy, 1959.

Deedy, John. *Eyes on the Modern World.* New York: P. J. Kenedy, 1965.

De la Bedoyere, Michael. *Objections to Roman Catholicism.* London: Constable, 1964.

De Lubac, Henri, S.J. *Catholicism: Social Aspectts of Dogma. A Study of Dogma in Relation to the Corporate Destiny of Mankind.* New York: Sheed and Ward, 1958.

――― *The Splendour of the Church.* Glen Rock, N. J.: Deus Books, Paulist Press, 1963.

Dondeyne, A. *Contemporary European Thought and Christian Faith.* Pittsburgh: Duquesne U. Press, 1958.

Ellis, John Tracy. *American Catholicism.* Chicago: University of Chicago Press, 1956.

Folliet, Joseph. *World Catholicism Today.* Westminster, Md.: Newman, 1961.

Graham, Dom Aelred. *Catholicism and the World Today.* New York: McKay, 1952.

Guardini, R. *The Faith and Modern Man.* London: Burns and Oates, 1951.

Gurian, Waldermar and Fitzsimmons, Mark A. (eds.). *The Catholic Church in World Affairs.* Notre Dame: Notre Dame University Press, 1954.

Hales, E.E.Y. *The Catholic Church in the Modern World.* New York: Hanover House, 1958.

Harbinson, E. Harris. *Christianity and History*. Princeton U. Press, 1964.
Love, Thomas T. *John Courtney Murray: Contemporary Church-State Theory*. Garden City, N.Y.: Doubleday, 1965.
Mascall, E. L. *The Secularization of Christianity*. New York: Holt, Rinehart and Winston, 1965.
Ong, Walter, S.J. *American Catholic Crossroads: Religious-Secular Encounters in the Modern World.*. New York: Collier, 1959.
Rommen, Heinrich. *The State in Catholic Thought*. St. Louis: Herder and Herder, 1945.
Suhard, Emmanuel. *The Church Today. Growth or Decline?* 5th ed. Notre Dame Ind.: Fides, 1960.
Sturzo, Luigi. *Church and State*. London: Longmans, 1939.
Ward, Barbara. *Nationalism and Ideology*. New York: Norton, 1966.
Weigel, Gustave. *The Modern God: Faith in a Secular Culture*. New York: Macmillan, 1963.

3. Person and the Community of Man

D'Arcy, Martin, S.J. *Communism and Christianity*. New York: Devin-Adair, 1957.
———— *Mirage and Truth*. New York: Macmillan, 1935.
De Lubac, Henry, S.J. *The Drama of Atheist Humanism*. New York: Sheed and Ward, 1950.
Guardini, Romano. *Power and Responsibility*. Chicago: Regnery, 1961.
Maritain, Jacques. *The Person and the Common Good*. New York: Scribner.
———— *True Humanism*. London: Bles, 1946.
Messner, Johannes. *Social Ethics*. (Translated by J.J. Doherty. Rev. ed.) St. Louis: Herder, 1965.
Murray, John Courtney, S.J. *We Hold These Truths*. New York: Sheed and Ward, 1960.
Reinhold, H.A., James Collins, John Courtney Murray, Edward Duff, John LaFarge, W. Norris Clarke. "Symposium on Christian Humanism." *Social Order*. Vol. III, Nos. 5 and 6. May-June 1953.
Teilhard de Chardin, Pierre. *The Divine Milieu*. New York: Harper, 1960.

4. Religious Freedom

Cogley, John, ed. *Religion in America*. Cleveland: Meridian Paperback, 1960.
D' Arcy, Eric. *Conscience and Its Right to Freedom*. New York: Sheed & Ward, 1961.
de Albornez, A.F. Carullo. *Roman Catholicism and Religious Liberty*. World Council of Churches, 1959.
Janssen, Louis. *Freedom of Conscience and Religious Freedom*. New York: Alba House.
Küng, Hans. *Freedom Today*. New York: Sheed and Ward, 1965.
Murray, John Courtney, S.J. *The Problem of Religious Freedom*. Westminster, Md.: Newman, 1965.

O'Neill, James. *Catholicism and American Freedom.* New York: Harpers, 1952.

Parsons, Wilfred, S.J. *The First Freedom.* New York: Macmillan, 1948.

5. The Family

Barbeau, Clayton C. *Head of the Family.* Chicago: Regnery, 1961.

Barrett, Donald (ed.). *The Problem of Population.* Notre Dame U. Press, 1964.

Callahan, Sydney. *Illusion of Eve.* New York: Sheed and Ward, 1965.

Dupre, Louis. *Contraception and Catholics. A New Appraisal.* Baltimore: Helicon, 1964.

Firkel, Eva. *Woman in the Modern World.* Notre Dame, Ind.: Fides, 1956.

Grisez, Germain. *Contraception and the Natural Law.* Milwaukee: Bruce, 1964.

Häring, Bernard. *Marriage in the Modern World.* Westminster, Md.: The Newman Press, 1966.

Leclercq, Jacques. *Marriage and the Family: A Study in Social Philosophy.* Cincinnati: Pustet, 1949.

Moran, William E. *Population Growth — Threat to Peace.* New York: P. J. Kenedy, 1965.

Noonan, John T. *Contraception: A History of its Treatment by the Catholic Theologians and Canonists.* Cambridge: Harvard University Press, 1965.

Sheed, Frank J. *Marriage and the Family.* New York: Sheed & Ward, 1957.

Thomas, John L., S.J. *The American Catholic Family.* New York: Prentice Hall, 1956.

————— *Catholic Viewpoint on Marriage and the Family.* Rev. ed. Garden City, N. Y.: Doubleday, 1965.

Woods, Sister Frances Jerome. *The American Family System.* N. Y.: Harper, 1959.

6. Cultural Development and Catholic Education

Barzun, Jacques. *The House of Intellect.* New York: Harper, 1959.

Bouyer, Louis, C. O. *Christian Humanism.* Westminster, Md.: Newman, 1959.

Christ, Frank L. and Gerard Sherry. *American Catholicism and the Intellectual Ideal.* New York: Appleton, 1959.

Cochrane, Charles N. *Christianity and Classical Culture.* New York: Oxford, 1940.

Danforth Commission on Church Colleges and Universities. *Eight Hundred Colleges Face the Future.* St. Louis: The Danforth Foundation, 1965.

Dawson, Christopher. *The Crisis in Western Education.* New York: Sheed and Ward, 1961.

————— *The Crisis of Western Education.* New York: Sheed and Ward, 1964.

―――― *The Historic Reality of Christian Culture.* New York: Harper, 1960.
―――― *Religion and the Rise of Western Culture.* New York: Sheed and Ward, 1950.
Donovan, John D. *The Academic Man in the Catholic College.* New York: Sheed and Ward, 1964.
Maritain, Jacques. *Education at the Crossroads.* New Haven: Yale, 1943.
―――― *Religion and Culture.* New York-London: Sheed and Ward, 1935.
McDonald, Donald, and others. *The Moral Curve.* New York: America Press, 1961.
McGucken, William J. S.J. *Catholic Education.* New York: America Press, 1955.
Murphy, Joseph S. (ed.) *Christianity and Culture.* Baltimore: Helicon, 1960.
Newman, John Henry Cardinal. *The Idea of a University.* New York: Longmans, Green, 1947.
O'Dea, Thomas F. *American Catholic Dilemma.* New York: Sheed and Ward, 1958.
Ong, Walter, S.J. *Frontiers in American Catholicism.* New York: Macmillan, 1957.
Pius XII. *Pius XII and Catholic Education.* St. Meinrad, Ind.: Grail, 1957.
Shuster, George. *Education and Moral Wisdom.* New York: Harper, 1960.
"The Contemporary University: U. S. A." *Daedalus.* Fall, 1964.
Van Doren, Mark. *Liberal Education.* Boston: Beacon Press, 1959.
Ward, Lew, C. S. C. *Exploring a Theology of Education.* Milwaukee: Bruce, 1950.

7. Social and Economic Development

Calvez, Jean-Yves. *The Social Thought of John XXIII.* Chicago: Regnery, 1959.
Calvez, Jean-Yves, S.J., and Perrin, Jacques. *The Church and Social Justice: Papal Social Teaching from Leo XIII to Pius XII.* Chicago: Regnery, 1961.
Chenu, M.D. *A Theology of Work.* London: Burns and Oates, 1956. French edition: *Pour une Theologie du Travail.* Paris: Editions de Seuil, 1955.
Cronin, John F. *Christianity and Social Progress: A Commentary on Mater et Magistra.* Baltimore: Helicon, 1965.
Greeley, Andrew M. *The Church and the Suburbs.* New York: Sheed and Ward, 1959.
Gremillion, Joseph. *The Other Dialogue.* New York: Doubleday, 1965.
Harrington, Michael. *The Other American.* New York: Macmillan, 1963.
―――― *The Accidental Century.* New York: Macmillan, 1965.
Jackson, Sir Robert G. A. *The Case for an International Development Authority.* Syracuse, N. Y.: Syracuse University Press, 1959.

McCormack, Arthur. *World Poverty and the Christian*. New York: Hawthorn Books, 1963.

Millikan, Max F., and Blackmer, David L.M. *The Emerging Nations. Their Growth and United States Policy*. Boston: Little, Brown, 1961.

Moody, Joseph N., and Lawler, J. George (eds.). *The Challenge of Mater et Magistra*. New York: Herder and Herder, 1963.

Rostow, W. W. *The Stages of Economic Growth*. Cambridge, England: Cambridge University Press, 1960.

Stanford Research Institute. *Significant Issues in Economic Aid*. Menlo Park, California: International Industrial Development Center, 1960.

Ward, Barbara. *The Rich Nations and the Poor Nations*. New York: Norton, 1962.

Gilson, Etienne (ed.). *The Church Speaks to the Modern World. The Social Teachings of Leo XIII*. Garden City, N.Y.: Doubleday, 1954.

8. Political Development

Almond, Gabriel A., and Verba, Sidney. *Civic Culture*. Boston: Little, Brown, 1965.

Apter, David E. *The Politics of Modernization*. Chicago: University of Chicago Press, 1965.

Caponigri, A. *The Church and the Political Order*. New York: Harper and Row.

Georner, E. A. *Peter and Caesar*. St. Louis: Herder and Herder, 1966.

Guardini, Romano. *Power and Responsibility. A Course of Action for the New Age*. Chicago: Regnery, 1961.

Hallowell, John H. *Main Currents in Modern Political Thought*. New York: Holt, Rinehart, and Winston, 1950.

Horowitz, Irving Louis. *Three Worlds of Development. The Theory and Practice of International Stratification*. New York: Oxford University Press, 1966.

Kautsky, John H. *Political Change in Underdeveloped Countries*. New York: John Wiley, 1962.

Maritain, Jacques. *Man and the State*. Chicago: Phoenix, 1951.

Organski, A.F.K. *The Stages of Political Development*. New York: Knopf, 1965.

Simon, Yves. *The Philosophy of Democratic Government*. Chicago: University of Chicago Press, 1951.

9. War and Peace

American Academy of Arts and Science. "Conditions of World Order" *Daedalus*. Spring, 1966.

Batchelder, Robert C. *The Irreversible Decision, 1939–1950*. New York: Macmillan, 1965.

Bennett, John C. *Foreign Policy in Christian Perspective*. New York: Scribner's Sons, 1966.

Boyd, Andrew. *United Nations, Piety, Myth and Truth*. New York: Pelican Paperback, 1962.

Clancy, William (ed.). *The Moral Dilemma of Nuclear Weapons*. New York: Council on Religion and International Affairs, 1961.

Constitution for the World (Peace Paper Series). Santa Barbara: Center for the Study of Democratic Institutions.

deSoras, Alfred, S.J. *International Morality.* New York: Hawthorn Books, 1963.

Finn, James (ed.). *Peace, the Churches and the Bomb.* New York: Council on Religion and International Affairs, 1965.

Flannery, Harry (ed.). *Pattern for Peace. Catholic Statements on International Order.* Westminster, Md.: Newman Press, 1962.

Gardner, Richard N. *In Pursuit of World Order.* New York: Praeger, 1964.

Hutchins, Robert. *St. Thomas and the World State.* Milwaukee: Marquette, 1949.

Leclercq, Jacques. *The Christian and World Integration.* New York: Hawthorn, 1963.

Millis, Walter, and John C. Murray, S.J. *Foreign Policy and the Free Society.* New York: Oceana, 1958.

Monks of Solesme (ed.). *Papal Teachings.* Boston: Daughters of St. Paul, 1959.

Murray, Thomas E. *Nuclear Policy for War and Peace.* Cleveland: World, 1960.

Nagle, William J. (ed.). *Morality and Modern Warfare.* Baltimore: Helicon, 1960.

Ramsey, Paul. *War and the Christian Conscience.* Durham: Duke University Press, 1961.

Regemey, P. *Non Violence et Conscience Chretienne.* Paris: Editions du Cerf, 1958.

Riga, Peter. *Peace on Earth. A Commentary on Pope John's Encyclical.* New York: Herder and Herder, 1964.

Shuster, George N. *Cultural Cooperation and the Peace.* Milwaukee: Bruce, 1953.

Stein, Walter. (ed.). *Nuclear Weapons: A Catholic Response.* New York: Sheed and Ward, 1961.

Wadsworth, James. *The Glass House.* New York: Praeger, 1966.

10. The Layman

Alonso, Arthur. *Catholic Action and the Laity.* St. Louis: B. Herder, 1961.

Callahan, Daniel, (ed.). *Generation of the Third Eye.* New York: Sheed and Ward. 1965.

———— *The Mind of the Catholic Layman.* New York: Scribner, 1963.

Congar, Yves, O.P. *Lay People in the Church.* (trans. by Donald Attwater.) Westminster, Md.: Newman Press, 1965.

de la Bedoyere, Michael. *The Layman in the Church.* London: Burns, Oates and Washbourne, 1955.

Fichter, Joseph, S.J. *Priest and People.* New York: Sheed and Ward, 1965.

Firkel, Eva. *Woman in the Modern World.* Notre Dame: Fides, 1956.

Gerken, John D. *Towards a Theology of the Layman.* New York: Herder and Herder, 1963.

Guitton, Jean. *The Church and the Laity.* New York: Alba House, 1965.

Knox, Ronald. *The Layman and His Conscience*. New York: Sheed and Ward, 1961.

Leclercq, Jacques. *Christians in the World*. New York: Sheed and Ward, 1961.

Mouroux, Jean. *The Meaning of Man*. New York: Sheed and Ward, 1948.

Newman, Jeremiah. *The Christian in Society*. Baltimore: Helicon, 1962.

Newman, John Henry. *On Consulting the Faithful in Matters of Doctrine*. New York: Sheed and Ward, 1962.

O'Gara, James (ed.). *The Layman in the Church*. New York: Herder and Herder, 1962.

Phillips, Gerard. *The Role of the Laity in the Church*. Chicago: Fides, 1955.

Rahner, Karl, S.J. *Free Speech in the Church*. New York: Sheed and Ward, 1959.

Schillebeeckx, Edward, O.P. *The Layman in the Church*. New York: Alba House, 1963.

Tavard, George. *The Church, the Layman and the Modern World*. New York: Macmillan, 1959.

Ward, Les (ed.). *The American Apostolate*. Westminster, Md.: Newman, 1952.

World Crisis and the Catholic. New York: Sheed and Ward, 1958.

11. American Catholicism

Doty, William L. *Trends and Counter Trends among American Catholics*. St. Louis: B. Herder, 1962.

Ellis, John T. *Perspectives in American Catholicism*. Baltimore: Helicon, 1964.

Herr, Dan and Wells, Joel. *Through Other Eyes*. Westminster, Md.: Newman, 1965.

Keating, Edward. *The Scandal of Silence*. New York: Random, 1965.

MacEoin, Gary. *New Challenges to American Catholics*. New York: Kenedy, 1965.

MacDonald, Donald. *Catholics in Conversation*. Philadelphia: Lippincott, 1960.

McAvoy, Thomas T., CSC (ed.). *Roman Catholicism and the American Way of Life*. Notre Dame U. Press, 1960.

Putz, Louis J. (ed.). *The Catholic Church: U.S.A.* Chicago: Fides, 1956.

Scharper, Philip (ed.). *American Catholics: A Protestant and Jewish View*. New York: Sheed and Ward, 1959.

Shuster, George et al. *Catholicism in America*. New York: Harcourt Brace, 1954.

INDEX

169

LC

Date Due

MAR 1 5 '68	CANISIUS	NOV 2 7 '73 CANISIUS	
MAY 2 0 '68	CANISIUS		
AUG 7 '68	CANISIUS		
NOV 1 8 '68	CANISIUS		
MAR 9 '70	CANISIUS		
MAY 6 '74	CANISIUS		